THE WOMEN WHO FOUNDED RISD

NANCY AUSTIN

DEDICATION

To the wise women and men of Rhode Island - across generations past, present, and still to come.

To RISD founder Helen Adelia Rowe Metcalf and her remarkable biography, still untold.

To the memory of my parents.

To my children: Caroline Woolard and Cyrus Woolard.

ABOUT THE AUTHOR

NANCY AUSTIN is a design historian, educator, and leadership coach based in Newport, Rhode Island. Since the early 1990s Dr. Austin has spoken internationally about the history of the Rhode Island School of Design (RISD) and published on this subject. Her Brown University PhD thesis on the history of RISD was among the first in the United States to tackle the meaning ecology of art and design in the nineteenth century, and chase its legacy into the twenty-first century. Nancy Austin taught the history of art and design from 1985 to 2008 at WPI, RISD, and Yale. After 2008 her work shifted out from the academy toward public history engagement, exploring new ways for cultural institutions to lead with new stories leveraging new tech platforms for global impact. Nancy Austin is CEO of Leonardo Coaching and an Innovation Women speaker. Follow her on Facebook at Nancy Austin | Studio Austin Alchemy.

The Women Who Founded RISD

By Nancy A. Austin, PhD

"What a *beginning* is worth":

The Women's Centennial Committee of Rhode Island

and the Founding of RISD, 1875-1877

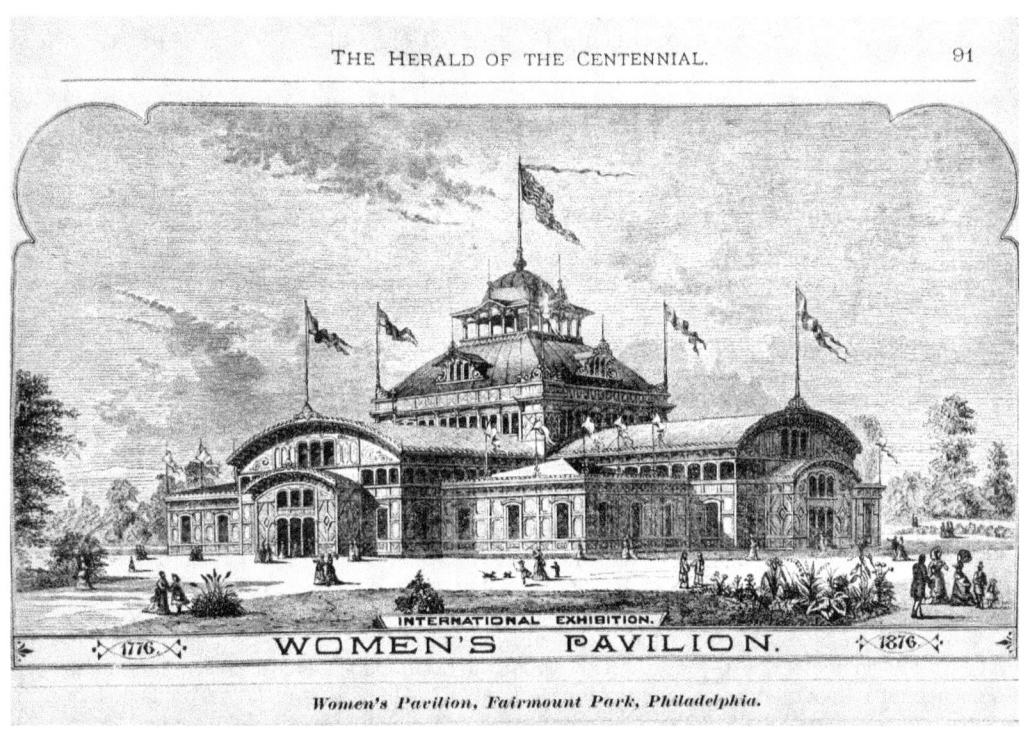

Women's Pavilion, Fairmount Park, Philadelphia.

1. The Women's Pavilion at the 1876 Centennial Exhibition, as illustrated in the RI newspaper written and published by RI women – including Helen Rowe Metcalf.

"When the first little wave of the rising tide comes creeping up the shore, the sun derides her, and the dry sand drinks her, and her frightened sisters pull her backward, and yet again she escapes; and still her expostulating sisters cling to her skirts, and the rabble of waves behind cry out against her boldness, and all the depths of ocean seem rising to drag her down. And now the second rank of waves, who would have died of shame at being the first, have unwittingly passed the earlier mark of the little wave that led them; and now you may float your ships, for lo, the tide is full."

[Quote from: *New Century for Women* (May 13, 1876), 4, the newspaper published at the 1876 World's Fair Women's Pavilion. That exhibition hall was built with funds contributed by the RI Women's Centennial Commission]

Introduction[1]

The idea of RISD was born in Mrs. Nancy Sackett's parlor on January 11th, 1877.[2] On that cold Thursday morning, almost four dozen members of the Rhode Island Women's Centennial Commission gathered on the West Side of Providence to decide what to do with the $1500 remaining in their treasury.[3] The women had come together two years earlier to raise money and enthusiasm for the upcoming world's fair, or Centennial Exposition - planned for Philadelphia in 1876. Unexpectedly, they had become consummate fundraisers. Rhode Islanders had flocked to their first event, a Martha Washington Tea Party. But this was nothing compared to the crowd of almost nine thousand that gathered to see their re-creation of the 1772 burning of the British schooner, the *Gaspee*, at Mashapaug Pond.[4] After such a successful beginning, the RI women were quick to pledge $3000 to the national Women's Centennial Commission when each state was asked to help finance a separate Women's Pavilion to showcase women's work at the world's fair.

However, after a year of avid fund-raising, the RI Centennial women had turned away from any sense of shared sisterhood with the national headquarters in Philadelphia and set off on their own

---

[1] This research was first presented to the *American Seminar* at the John Nicholas Brown Center, Brown University, on October 23, 2002. My work on the Centennial women was prompted by the March 20, 2002 *Founders Forum* symposium on the women who founded RISD. Entitled "Daughters of Invention", it was organized by RISD Dean Dawn Barrett and brought together a critical mass of people interested in the continuing relevance of RISD's history. At the symposium, it struck me that the trajectory of historical writing on the founding women's accomplishments had overstepped the known facts. Practically nothing was known about these women or their actual role in starting the school. Bronson's few comments were vague and ambiguous in her unpublished, reliable workhorse history of RISD's first fifty years. I set out to document who these women were and what they did and did not do. I could begin this project because of the excellent state of the RISD Archives, under the ever-helpful direction of Andrew Martinez and Douglas Doe. Among other things, they helped me set up a database to manage the vast roster of people and connections that I encountered each day in my research. A breakthrough came when Richard D. Statler, Manuscripts Curator at the RI Historical Society, rediscovered the RI Centennial Women's bound manuscript Records, or book of minutes, after Andrew Martinez found the tiny newspaper clipping in a RISD scrapbook that proved these Records had been donated to the RIHS in 1902. Since then, I have used other sources to place this document in a larger context. For example, I did extensive archival research in Philadelphia on the national Centennial Women and this completely changed my understanding of the RI women's actions.
[2] Eliza S. Manchester, "Records, Women's Centennial Executive Committee," Rhode Island Historical Society. (Hereafter cited as Records MS).
[3] After discovering the book of minutes on April 24, 2002, I released an early account of the founding of the school on April 29,2002. A version of this was published in the Fall 2002 issue of *RISD Views*. The Records MS very clearly states that in January 1877 the Centennial women were debating what to do with $1500, not $1675. This latter figure is the actual, final amount that was deposited into RISD's account in May 1877.
[4] With pride, Rhode Islanders believe the burning of the Gaspee is the "first blow struck for American freedom" in the war for Independence. To appreciate the scale of this Centennial Women's event, see the Saturday morning edition of the *Providence Journal*, June 12, 1875. Over 250 Centennial women were involved at this point. Also, one could point to this dramatic spectacle of burning a boat on the water (illuminated by Chinese lanterns, locomotive headlights, and rocket flares) as a historic precedent for the contemporary *Waterfire* public engagement event that captivates the public today.

independent path. Even before the world's fair opened, the RI women had stopped sending money to Philadelphia, and maintained a significant balance in their own treasury. Now, with the world's fair over, the RI Centennial women were at Mrs. Sackett's house on Pine Street in the jewelry district that January morning to attend to unfinished business and disband. The most pressing issue was how to appropriate the $1500 remaining in their treasury.[5] What kind of follow-up could commemorate their successes?

As discussion got underway at Mrs. Sackett's, it became clear that $1500 was a sum both *too small* to accomplish a grand vision and yet signified something *too large* to devote to a mere memorial. The first proposals were to put the money in some kind of trust that would accrue interest for one hundred years and in this way, turn into a sum large enough to be used meaningfully. The second concept was an achievable project and proved popular: why not commission an architectural drinking fountain for the new Roger Williams Park being designed on the West Side of Providence? The fountain could complement the one RI Centennial Women Anna Richmond had endowed for $600 in 1873 as a civic-minded perimeter gesture for the Providence Athenaeum on the East Side of Providence.[6]

2. The RI Centennial Women ultimately chose institution building over endowing an architectural drinking fountain. The fountain's planned site was the new 427-acre Roger Williams Park – recently gifted to the city on the West Side. We can imagine the drinking fountain concept as a complement to this granite one in front of the Providence Athenaeum on Benefit St., on the East Side. Centennial Woman Anna Richmond had endowed the Athenaeum fountain for $600 in 1873; it was designed by architects Ware and Van Brunt and remains today a place-making icon.

---

[5] Between May 1876 and the meeting at Mrs. Sackett's house, the group had spent about $1000, leaving a balance of $1588.57.
[6] Jane Lancaster, *Inquire Within* (2003): 90-3. The granite drinking fountain was designed by Boston architects Ware and Van Brunt. $300 was set aside for the expense of upkeep. Lancaster notes this was "one of thirty Providence fountains connected to the new Pawtuxet water supply." Although the Providence Athenaeum did not have a water supply until July 1875. Roger Williams Park was gifted to the City in 1871 and designed in 1878. Anna (Mrs. George) Richmond was an active RI Centennial Woman. For more on Anna Eddy Richmond (1810-1881) and her son, the artist Walter Richmond (1839-1912) as art collectors impacting Providence, see: Nancy Austin, "The Half-Life and After-Life of New Media," (Nov. 2015) *Journal of Contemporary Archival Studies*, Vol. 2, Article 3, (November 2015), 20-23. [http://elischolar.library.yale.edu/jcas/vol2/iss2/3]

When both the trust proposals and the fountain memorial failed to win a majority of votes, Helen Adelia Rowe Metcalf offered an alternative that combined century-long vision and pragmatism: why not use the money <u>now</u> as seed money to start an art or design school in Providence? Surely, community support would follow. Although a majority supported Mrs. Metcalf's idea, the women decided to vote by ballot. The tally was as follows:

School of Design	20 votes
Drinking Fountain	10
Public Library	9
Brown University	3
Charity	3
Art Gallery & Library	1

These results triggered a run-off ballot between the proposal for a "School of Design" and that for a "Drinking Fountain". The women voted that the results of this run-off vote would be final. The "School of Design" won by a vote of 34 to 13. Institution building it would be! ... But this was not the end of decision making.

In the weeks that followed, front-page editorials and letters to the editor ran in the *Providence Journal* and *Evening Bulletin* urging the women to reconsider and pointing out the folly of throwing away this small amount of money on an endeavor that did not have the assurance of a trust legacy. Other letters wrote back supporting the proposed action. When the women met again on February 7th, Mrs. Metcalf made a resolution to reconsider the vote, but it was not acted upon. The Centennial Women concluded their activities on February 22, 1877 and disbanded - with the final entry in their "*Minutes*" a plea to history to remember their good faith in choosing to plant the seeds of a design school.

The Women's Centennial Commission did not, themselves, seek to implement their vision for a school of design. For this next step, they selected a Board of Trustees comprised primarily of prominent businessmen. Only three of the Centennial women chose to be members of the fund's Board, and one dropped out within a year. But the two who remained left an enduring legacy, especially Helen Rowe Metcalf. She was the 47-year old mother of five who had originally proposed the idea of a school of design. Helen Rowe Metcalf was a visionary and strategic coalition builder; without her ongoing leadership at its founding in the 1870s, RISD would not exist.

There is no doubt that the Women's Centennial Commission felt pride and ownership for laying a new foundation for a long-awaited design school in Providence. As the group's secretary, Eliza Manchester, wrote in a front-page newspaper article: "We all know what a *beginning* is worth – that a nucleus soon draws to itself what is necessary to its successful growth. Our $1500 shall be that nucleus. Will not the lovers of art in Providence supply the material which shall make its completeness?"

"What a *beginning* is worth". A critic wrote back and pointed out the folly of her logic. Manchester had described this new 1870s plan as a continuation of earlier efforts in the 1850s by the Rhode Island Art Association. But these plans had come to naught and indeed sacrificed a founding trust established by Rhode Island architect Thomas Tefft (1826-59). The critic argued that the women's money would be lost as well, and begged them to be more conservative.

The critic's concern was justified, and credit for RISD's early survival goes in part to the early members of the Board of Trustees. Without their executive ability to seek coalition-building between diverse stakeholders (such as artists and designers, reformers and manufacturers, private and public funding initiatives) then nothing would have come of the Centennial Women's vision. But without the women's beginning assertion to be institution builders, there is no story at all.

Thus, this is the story of how the women came to be in Mrs. Sackett's parlor that cold January 11th morning in 1877. Why did these women, unlike all the other Centennial women in the United States, decide to found a design school, and name it after the whole state?

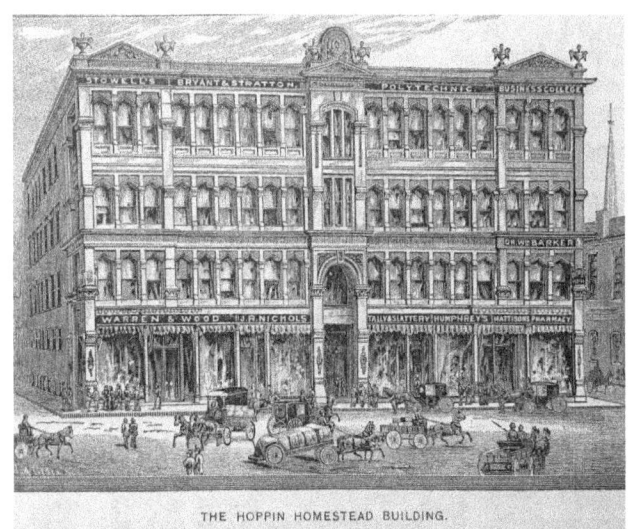

THE HOPPIN HOMESTEAD BUILDING.

3. From October 1878 to 1893, the Rhode Island School of Design held classes on the top floor of the Hoppin Homestead Building, located in downtown Providence on Westminster St. between Snow and Aborn St. (The building was demolished in the 20th c. and is now a parking lot, behind AS220.) The building was built in 1876 and served as an innovation incubator for education-minded experiments, including a new business college, a language institute, and the Rhode Island Institute of Technology – alongside the new design school. RISD only moved to the East Side Waterman Building (across from the Providence Art Club) in 1893 in order to win the Jones Bequest lawsuit.

March 1876: The Turning Point

Until March 1876, there was nothing unusual about the RI chapter of the national Women's Centennial Committee. The RI chapter had been formed somewhat later than other states, but quickly redeemed itself.[7] With a flurry of fundraising from January 1875 to February 1876, the RI women from this small state raised over $10,000 and surprisingly became the fifth largest state contributor to the national office.

What happened in March 1876, then, to so decisively turn the allegiance of the RI women away from the goals of the national committee and set them on the path that unexpectedly led to the founding of RISD? At the end of February, the WCC-RI had voted to continue financing their local newspaper, *Herald of the Century*, but in early April it was unanimously decided not to subsidize the newspaper any longer.[8] No more fundraisers were planned by the WCC-RI after March. They let the lease expire on the rented rooms in the Fletcher Building in downtown Providence where the women had been meeting. Suddenly the goal was to wrap up loose ends and disband, despite the opportunities to unite further under this, or other, organizational umbrellas.[9] As we will see, the events of March 1876 not only severed the group's sense of allegiance to the national organization but also point to unspoken interstate rivalries between the Centennial committees in the different RI cities.

The most important cause of this abrupt disaffection in March 1876 was heightened alarm over the leadership style and ambition of the national head of the Women's Centennial, Mrs. Elizabeth Duane Gillespie. An accomplished political operative, Mrs. Gillespie had organized the women in Philadelphia and Pennsylvania hierarchically to create an effective "party machine"; members were subdivided into local Ward chapters and sent out to each factory and home in the district to solicit membership. This pattern was supposed to be duplicated in every state that reported to her. But Rhode Island is geographically small and organizing women by political Ward failed to meet the networking needs of the RI women and how they understood affiliation.[10] The Rhode Island women coalesced around their shared distinctive state identity.

---

[7] In August 1873, the national committee appointed Elizabeth Goddard to chair the RI state branch, but no RI planning committee meetings were held until January 1875. The first open organizational meeting for the women of the state was held at Goddard's house on January 25, 1875; about 100 women attended.

[8] Records MS, February 28 and April 4, 1876. It is worth noting that if the women had agreed to continue subsidizing the money-losing newspaper venture until the end of the Centennial, there probably would not have been any surplus money with which to found RISD.

[9] The exception to this is the exclusive RI Woman's Club.

[10] Records MS, April 5, 1875.

4. Mrs. Gillespie, at the national headquarters of the Women's Centennial Committee receiving reports from her sub-committees.

MRS. GILLESPIE IN MARTHA WASHINGTON COSTUME,
TEA-PARTY, DECEMBER, 1873

5. Mrs. Gillespie dressed for the Martha Washington Tea Party, 1873.

Gillespie also had a fairly-militant feminist agenda that she was uncannily able to advance without alienating men in power. This is usually attributed to Gillespie's demonstrated success at grassroots organizing. For example, with unusual political savvy, Gillespie had mobilized large numbers of women on a moment's notice to sell stock for the Centennial in the earliest, uncertain hours of its planning stages. She then parlayed this favor into being named national head of the Centennial Women, a paying job[11]. But Gillespie's ideological ambitions for the national Women's Centennial Commission and the landmark Women's Pavilion extended far beyond good cheer and fundraising. Gillespie was committed to helping women achieve economic self-sufficiency, and envisioned the Women's Pavilion as a showcase for the new livelihoods available to women through women's work in such fields as invention, medicine, journalism, and design.

In March 1876, Mrs. Gillespie sent two memos from her office in Philadelphia to the state chapters. Together, these memos reveal a flawed leader who combined vision and hubris. Both of Gillespie's memos completely outraged the RI women. First, they were shocked to learn that Mrs. Gillespie wanted more money from each State Committee to pay for guarding and maintaining the Women's Pavilion during the Centennial. They registered extreme disgust that *women* should be singled out and asked to take on an additional expense not required of other, larger buildings. They asked incredulously: "The ladies of the country are obliged to take care of their own building, cleansing, cleaning up etc. – After having raised $36,000 toward the erection of the Women's Pavilion they are to be taxed for the care of it."[12] It is possible this new requirement was demanded by the leaders of the US Centennial Commission, but it is more likely that it was integral to Mrs. Gillespie's plan to have the whole project run and funded entirely by women as a way of showcasing women's capacity for practical self-sufficiency. Gillespie wrote: "In reply to the question now so often asked, 'What further need have you for money?' we would say that we hope to bear all the expenses attending our exhibition ourselves. Our insurance, our watchmen, and our employees will all require money."[13] Indeed, this was the point remarked upon in a later *New York Tribune* article: "[The

---

[11] As the head of the Women's Department, the Centennial Commission since June 1874 had paid Mrs. Gillespie $75/month. Curran, citing the Minutes of the Centennial Finance Board. See: Ruth Curran, "The City of Sisterly Love", (Honors Thesis, Bryn Mawr College, 1989): 72-3. By comparison, the chief of the Art Bureau was paid $333.33/month, as were the heads of other Halls. The Chief of the Bureau of Machinery and the Director General received $666.66/month. (Box A-1542, Board of Finance Records, Philadelphia City Archives)

[12] Records MS, March 6,13 1876.

[13] "Women's Department. International Exhibition," *Third Annual Report of the Women's Centennial Executive Committee* (Philadelphia, 1876), 9.

Women's Pavilion] has surely rendered it impossible ever again to impugn woman's practical ability. She has shown conclusively that she is able to carry forward successfully anything she chooses to undertake, from the raising of $95,000 to aid her brothers in the dark, early days of Centennial preparation, to the erection and furnishing of her own industrial domain managed entirely by herself, even to the function of engineer."[14] By March 1876, Mrs. Gillespie's confidence and ambitions had risen to unparalleled heights. In the *Third Annual Report*, written that month, she described the Centennial Women as an international organization of women that would change the future course of women's history:

> Success is now so evident that we offer our congratulations to our co-workers in this country, and to the women in foreign countries who have come up to help us show to the world, the good which may in future years be accomplished by women. At the same time, only the first steps are taken towards this object. The earth is but removed, preparatory to laying the foundation for a work, which we trust will be carried to completion by those who are to follow us, and that women, led to earn their livelihood in branches of business yet unknown to them, will have reason to bless the organization known now as the Women's Centennial Executive Committee.[15]

The second memo that Mrs. Gillespie sent to the States simply reached too far. The RI women took it as incontrovertible proof of Mrs. Gillespie's unbridled ambition and ego. At the same moment that Mrs. Gillespie's requested more money from the state committees to maintain the women-run Women's Pavilion, she came to them again with a new request for even *more* money to advance her strong personal commitment to music and music education in the United States. Somehow, Gillespie had hit upon the grandiose, off-message, and quixotic idea that the national Women's Centennial Committee should pay $5000 in solid gold to commission the "greatest living composer", Richard Wagner, to compose a "Centennial Inauguration March" for the general opening ceremonies of the World's Fair.[16] Gillespie had secured her favorite orchestra, The Theodore Thomas Orchestra, to perform this Wagnerian premiere. Unwilling to stop there, Gillespie was having her Philadelphia committee organize and pay for a show-stopping "chorus of one thousand voices" that would accompany this orchestra and a full organ in another opening ceremony musical performance of a hymn written by John Greenleaf Whittier.[17] (Indeed, Gillespie

---

[14] Reprinted in "Woman's Pavilion," *New Century* (August 19, 1876), 115.

[15] "Women's Department. International Exhibition," *Third Annual Report of the Women's Centennial Executive Committee* (Philadelphia, 1876), 5.

[16] The Women's Pavilion had a separate opening ceremony.

[17] Wagner did write the "American Centennial March" or "Grosser Festmarsch" (1876) as a commission from the WCC-US. The historian Brown reports that Wagner wrote to the conductor: "Whatever of melody or beauty there may be in it, is the inspiration of the beautiful ladies of America who made you their interpreter for me." See: Dee Brown, *The Year of the Century: 1876* (1966), 125. Citing Philadelphia *Public Ledger*, May 11, 1876. Brown states that the WCC

did accomplish all these goals; overall, the national women's committee allocated more than $7000 for "Centennial Music".[18])

But the RI women were not amused. Throughout March 1876, they discussed with dismay Gillespie's latest demand for them to pledge even more money to cover the cost of hiring the orchestra, Wagner's fee, and even perhaps Wagner's expenses if he would consent to leave Bayreuth and attend the premier. The tone-deaf hubris of this proposal seems to have been the final straw. In early March, Mrs. Goddard told the RI women that she would contact other State Chairs to see what they planned to do since it now seemed clear that "any protest they might make would be utterly lost unless sustained by the Centennial Committees of other States."[19] A week later, Mrs. Goddard could report that the women from Massachusetts had unanimously vetoed funding music for the general opening ceremonies.[20] After discussion, the RI women concurred that "we shall not pay Mr. Thomas or any other man for music at Philadelphia."[21]

It is against the backdrop of this unfolding drama over the scale of Mrs. Gillespie's ambitions for the national organization that the WCC-RI secretary noted at the end of March that the Pawtucket, RI Committee had just sent Mrs. Gillespie $1500 to fund the construction of a prototype preschool "Kindergarten" as an annex to the Women's Pavilion.[22] This is interesting for several reasons. It is essentially the only mention in the WCC-RI Minutes of the Kindergarten, which proved to be a popular

---

paid $5000. He quotes the reactions at the premier as ranging from "brilliant, spirited, dashing, with reminders of Tristan and Isolde" to "no American theme" to "a dead failure". However, the historian Maass spins it that Wagner said the best thing about the Centennial March was the money he received for writing it. See: John Maass, *The Glorious Enterprise* (1973), 41. In her *Remembrances*, Gillespie merely notes that the March was "one of the gifts of the women". See: Mrs. E.D. Gillespie, *A Book of Remembrances*, 2nd ed. (1901), 328. She emphasizes instead her work organizing the chorus for the hymn written by Whittier to music by John K. Paine at the "urging" of Bayard Taylor. This piece was performed in the central transept of the Main Building accompanied by a full organ, orchestra, and chorus of 1000 voices. (Gillespie, 317-318; Brown,126; *WCC-US Final Report*, 11.)
[18] "Treasurer's Report, from November 10, 1875, to March 22, 1877." *WCC-US Final Report*, 34. Cordato states that Wagner was paid his fee in gold. See: Mary Francis Cordato, "Towards a New Century," *The Pennsylvania Magazine* (January 1983), 117.
[19] Records MS, March 6, 1876.
[20] Records MS, March 13, 1876.
[21] Records MS, March 13, 1876. Mrs. Gillespie returned to her music education advocacy with similarly disastrous effect at the end of the Centennial. Her first proposal for a national Centennial Women's Memorial advocated the legacy of a Music School. See below.
[22] Records MS, March 20, 1876.

success at the Centennial.[23] This novel approach to education generated quite a bit of publicity at the World's Fair, and it was often noted that the women of Pawtucket, RI had funded it[24].

The Pawtucket Committee's independent fundraising and apparently autonomous decision to fund a Kindergarten is an important example that must alert us to the interstate dynamics of the WCC-RI. We know that another RI Committee, the Warwick and Coventry Committee retained the money from its own fundraising until as late as 1880, when they finally donated it to RISD.[25] The story of the Kindergarten documents the relative independence of some of the city organization within RI, and the predominately Providence focus of WCC-RI, which gathered within it women who identified with the metropolitan center but might live in other towns, such as East Greenwich. Thus, not only was the WCC-RI only partially embedded in the national hierarchy, but it also had a strong Providence bias.[26] Within the state, it appears there was a degree of autonomy, and perhaps even competition, between the committees.[27] It is not clear how much overlapping there might have been in the final voting on how to allocate the WCC-RI funds. It is possible that only Providence, or Providence-affiliated women were there. Regardless, the design school's intended umbrella was the whole state.

By supporting a new kind of educational initiative with the Kindergarten, the Pawtucket Committee revealed a different understanding of the goal of the Women's Department than was shown by Providence. (As we will see, the WCC-RI did not fully embrace the ideological mission of the Women's Pavilion, as revealed in the work participating women chose to send.) The Froebel Kindergarten idea that the Pawtucket women funded had been known in the United States since the late 1840s, but the first "successful" one had been introduced to immigrant children in St. Louis in 1873, in the hopes of imparting middle-class virtues

---

[23] The Records MS, January 10, 1876, does mention: "Letter received from Mrs. Wm. D. Ely in regard to Kindergarten". But that is all.

[24] "Women's Department. International Exhibition," *Third Annual Report of the Women's Centennial Executive Committee* (Philadelphia, 1876), 9: "Besides this we have undertaken to bear the expense of a great Educational Exhibit, and are now erecting a building especially for Kindergarten schools, a work which peculiarly belongs to women. Our organization in Pawtucket, RI, requests that their contribution shall be appropriated to this branch of our work."

[25] Records MS, March 13, 1876 reported that both Warwick and Coventry had done fundraising.

[26] The first page of the Records MS says they are the "Records – Women's Centennial Executive Committee of Providence, RI."

[27] *The Herald of the Centennial* never mentions Pawtucket's funding of the Kindergarten. It does report on Mrs. Gillespie's decision to add the Kindergarten as an annex to the Women's Pavilion, and the ideology behind it. Other articles summarized the busy fundraising activities of the Pawtucket women from November 1875 through January 1876, but no mention is made of Pawtucket's decision to fund this structure. (*Herald of the Centennial*, 84-5, 91,92).

to the very young before these children abandoned all schooling to work, often by age ten.[28] The 1876 Women's Department Centennial demonstration proved to be the vehicle popularizing the idea of the Kindergarten in America.[29] For example, it was at this Women's Pavilion annex that Mrs. Wright (who had recently moved to Weymouth, Massachusetts from Pawtucket) learned about the Froebel blocks that she then bought for her nine-year old son, the future architect Frank Lloyd Wright.[30]

6. Exterior view of the prototype Kindergarten that the Pawtucket, RI Centennial Women helped fund as an annex to the Women's Pavilion at the 1876 Centennial.

---

[28] Michael Steven Shapiro, *Child's Garden: The Kindergarten Movement from Froebel to Dewey* (1983); Ann Taylor Allen, "Let us Live for our Children: Kindergarten Movements in Germany and the United States, 1840-1914," *History of Education Quarterly* 28 (Spring 1988), 22-48.

[29] There were five competing Kindergarten exhibitions at the Philadelphia World's Fair, but the Women's Department one proved most influential. See: Shapiro, 65-83, and Cordato, 128-129.

[30] Maass, 122-3, citing Grant Carpenter Manson, *Frank Lloyd Wright to 1910* (1958). See also: Robert C. Twombly, *Frank Lloyd Wright* (1979), 6-8,27. Grant Manson, "Wright in the Nursery; The Influence of Froebel Education on the Work of Frank Lloyd Wright," *The Architectural Review* 113 (June 1953); Stuart Wilson, "The 'Gifts' of Friedrich Froebel," *JSAH* 26 (December 1967). Twombly, 6-7 says father William C. Wright was the minister to the Pawtucket High St. Church from December 1871 to his resignation in January 1874. The family moved to Weymouth, MA that year, in September 1874. Mrs. Wright was not a RI Centennial woman and she was not the Weymouth Centennial Chair. (*Final Report*, 46.) See also: F.L. Wright, *An Autobiography* (1943), 11-16.

It is not known how the Pawtucket women came to the decision to support a Kindergarten. Perhaps the success of Pawtucket's efforts was an inspiration to the Centennial women who ended up voting to found a new school of design, which was itself a new kind of educational initiative. Education does not appear to be an interest of the WCC-RI at any time before the vote to found RISD. [31] For example, Providence-native Sarah Doyle was an early WCC-RI member and one of the three women who went on to be a founding Trustee of RISD. Doyle visited the world's fair and came home to lecture on the Educational Exhibits and new ideas in education that she had seen at the Centennial. But Doyle chose to present her findings to the RI Woman's Club, not the WCC-RI. [32] Pawtucket's role in funding the influential Centennial Prototype Kindergarten is another important legacy of the RI Centennial women. It serves as an example of women trying to effect change through new educational opportunities, and may have been an inspiration of sorts for the founding of RISD.

Despite Mrs. Gillespie's efforts and convictions, she failed to get any more money out of RI Centennial Committees after March 1876. Her disappointment at the WCC-RI's unwillingness to line up behind her national agenda is reflected in Mrs. Gillespie's accounts of the Centennial. The WCC-RI is barely mentioned in any of the national WCC literature or in Mrs. Gillespie's memoirs, *A Book of Remembrance*. This is surprising considering RI's early financial backing of the Women's Pavilion and final overall standing as the fifth-highest state contributor to the national WCC. [33] Instead, it is the Pawtucket funding of the Kindergarten that merits attention in Gillespie's accounts. [34] Indeed, the degree to which Gillespie ignores the WCC-RI is striking. For example, the two RI women who are documented as having traveled to the Women's Pavilion to install and remove the Rhode Island women's exhibits are omitted from the list of RI

---

[31] It is not clear that Sarah Doyle was an active member of the WCC-RI. The only references to Doyle in the records of the WCC-RI list her as an original member of the newspaper committee. (Records MS, February 8, 1875 and *Herald of the Centennial*, February 1875(1.1), 6).

[32] Doyle's lecture was October 4, 1876. See manuscript: "Secretary's First Record Book of Meetings of the Rhode Island Woman's Club, Jan. 16, 1878" in the Rhode Island Historical Society.

[33] Records MS, May 19, 1876. According to the WCC-US *Final Report*, 32 total donations to the national committee totaled $74,953.48. Historian Cordato, 117 states that the WCEC raised a total of $138,750 but this must include the sale of stock. The final order of highest-lowest State contributors is: 1) Pennsylvania: $15,176.80 with $11,522.50 from Philadelphia; 2) New York: $13,581; 3) Ohio: $10,908.05; 4) Massachusetts: $10,375; 5) RI: $4350 with Providence at $3000 and Pawtucket $1350; 6) New Jersey: $3156.29; 7) Connecticut: $2983.75; 8) New Hampshire: $2379.96; 9) Maine: $2379.08; 10) District of Columbia: $2025.04; 11) Vermont: $2000; 12) Illinois: $1000; 13) Maryland: $650; 14) California: $520.80; 15) Missouri: $175.46; 16) Kansas: $150; 17) Florida: 82.25; 18) Idaho:65; 19) Alabama: $20; 20) North Caroline: $20; 21) Indiana: $20; 22) Utah Territory: $10. There were 36 states in the USA in 1876.

[34] Gillespie, 322.

members published in Philadelphia's *Final Report*.[35] In Gillespie's chatty *Remembrances*, she describes a 1875 trip she took to visit the Women's Centennial Committees in Boston, Hartford, and New Haven, but she says nothing of her stop for a major presentation in Providence.[36] Her RI speech was attended by the US Centennial Commission Board of Finance member, John Gorham, and the US Commissioner from RI, Royal C. Taft; Mrs. Gillespie was hosted at a special dinner that was written up in the newspaper. But there is no special mention in her memoirs of the WCC-RI and its early, key support.

The events of March 1876 highlight the distinctive character of the Providence-based WCC-RI. The group differed subtly from other RI City committees, and, by the end, substantially from the goals and ambitions of the national Centennial Committee. The women of the WCC-RI simply failed to acquiesce to Mrs. Gillespie's style of leadership. Gillespie alienated the WCC-RI with her insistence on unquestioning allegiance to a hierarchical chain of authority. Partly this is an issue of regional culture and leadership style. Mrs. Gillespie was adored and supported until her death by a large group of women in Philadelphia.[37] But for the women of the WCC-RI, the model for successful leadership could not be built on a cult of personality or rigid hierarchy. Helen Rowe Metcalf's future effectiveness as a strategic coalition-building leader among the RI Centennial Women should be considered in this context.

The RI women did meet one more time in the spring of 1876 before adjourning until the end of the Centennial. With the rooms in the Fletcher building gone, the group's first attempts at a meeting were thwarted. The Secretary simply noted: "Meeting adjourned ... for want of a suitable place for holding it."[38] A few days later they held a culminating business meeting in the Ladies Parlor of Almy House. No mention

---

[35] Mrs. Shaw and Mrs. Cleveland. *Final Report*, 57,59. Compare to Records MS, April 14, 1876 and November 2, 1876.

[36] In her *Book of Remembrances*, Mrs. Gillespie devotes four pages to her meeting with the Boston Committee on April 18-19, 1875. The next short paragraph reads: "I made a brief visit to Hartford and New Haven on my way home .... At home, all was going smoothly." (Gillespie, 307-311.) Mrs. Gillespie spoke in Providence on April 22, 1875 at the Centennial Commission headquarters for RI. A dinner was held afterward at the home of Mrs. William Greene. (Records MS, April 22, 1875). See also: *Herald of the Centennial*, May 1875 (1.4), 28.

[37] At the end of the Centennial, the Philadelphia women used their own $3009.34 surplus budget as an outright gift to Mrs. Gillespie. (WCC-US *Final Report*, 34). However, the published Minutes of the final meeting of the WCC-US on March 22, 1877 state that other donations increased the amount given to Mrs. Gillespie at this time to $7,800. In presenting this money to Mrs. Gillespie, Mrs. Aubrey Smith claimed: "The Women's Centennial Committees of Boston, New York, and our own city, together with a number of the citizens of Philadelphia, desire to express their high appreciation of the work done by you in connection with the International Exhibition. ... " (Appendix No. 6, WCC-US *Final Report*, 90).

On her 75th birthday, a group of Philadelphia admirers gave her $18,000 that was invested for life so that she could live off the interest. Upon her death, the balance was to go to the Philadelphia School of Industrial Art for a ED Gillespie Scholarship. This school closed in 1964 and is now part of the University of the Arts. There is a Gillespie Scholarship at Bryn Mawr. (Newspaper clipping in the Hannah Zell Centennial Scrapbook, Archives, Philadelphia Museum of Art).

[38] Records MS, May 15, 1876.

was made of the opening of the Centennial nine days earlier; the focus of the meeting was to summarize the fundraising results of the last sixteen months of the group's existence.[39] The WCC-RI had raised $10,521.79 through "Sundry festivals", with expenses of $3,583.22.[40] Of that $6.938.57 profit, the group recorded that they sent $4350 to Philadelphia.[41] As the women prepared to wrap up their association, the WCC-RI treasury still carried a balance of $2588.57. It is noteworthy that the women spent $1000 between this point and the final tallying of accounts to see what was left to fund a new school of design.[42] With this summary of fundraising and Mrs. Goddard's bittersweet announcement that the RI women had been such generous contributors to the national WCC, the WCC-RI suspended its activities until the end of the World's Fair.

May-November 1876: Who went to the Centennial?

The Centennial Exhibition in Philadelphia was open for six months, from May 10th to November 10th, 1876. Recent historians have assumed the WCC-RI went as a delegation to the Centennial and came back galvanized to start a school of design.[43] However, known primary sources do not support this idea. Indeed, it seems that *few* of the Executive Committee, Ward or City Chairs, or general Centennial Committee members ever visited the Women's Pavilion. Is this possible?

---

[39] Records MS, May 19, 1876. They met at 4pm this time, instead of 11AM. Historian Blair states that most clubwomen were constrained to meet during the day and not in a public restaurant, so as not to risk their reputation. See Karen Blair, *The Clubwoman as Feminist* (1980), 62.

[40] This is a 66% profit rate.

[41] In the Minutes of this meeting, the Pawtucket Kindergarten fundraising and donation are included in the general WCC-RI report.

[42] Records MS, January 11, 1877 states that the women have $1500 remaining from their fundraising efforts. The approximately $1000 the WCC-RI spent to bring the women's exhibits home is close to the $1401.21 the NY Women's Centennial Committee set aside for this same task. ("Treasurers Report from the WCC-NY", *New Century*, May 20, 1876, 3.)

[43] This claim is not in Bronson or any early source. It is an important example of the need for a carefully documented history. Carla Mathes Woodward, "Acquisition,..." (1985), 11 seems to be the first source that implies that the RI women went to the Centennial: "At the Rhode Island exhibition of the Philadelphia Exposition of 1876, the Women's Centennial Commission, led by Mrs. Jesse Metcalf, was left with $1675 after meeting the exhibit's expenses; with this amount they determined to found the School of Design. A small sum, for a bold move". Bolger's *In Pursuit of Beauty*, 454 has a biography entry on Helen Metcalf that strengthens this to read: "Mrs. Metcalf, who headed the Women's Centennial Commission of the Rhode Island delegation to Philadelphia". McCarthy cites Bolger and makes many other factual errors. Burnham, 37 states that the women started RISD "directly following their visit to the Exhibition." Switzer, 136 writes: "Few records exist that satisfactorily describe the weight of feeling and accomplishment the women ... must have felt as they returned home".

7. The Women's Pavilion is glimpsed here to the far right amidst the other exhibition halls at the 1876 World's Fair.

8. Interior view of the Women's Pavilion.

The first source is the WCC-RI Minutes. They do not mention any Centennial visits, except for the separate votes in April and then November to have one or two women travel to Philadelphia to install, and then collect, the RI exhibition of women's work.[44] The group did not mention any plan to go to the opening ceremonies and, in fact, adjourned their activities for the duration of the Centennial.[45]

The second source is the "Register of Visitors to the Women's Department" which has survived for the four-month period July 10th to November 2nd, 1876.[46] A review of the approximately 7000 handwritten names listed there, with each person's home city and state noted, reveals that from July to November (about two-thirds of the total time the Fair was open) only about seven RI Centennial women visited the Women's Pavilion and signed the guest book.[47] Of these, three were active members, and two already had presented themselves in this research project as women likely to have been at the meeting where RISD was created.[48] Thus, we know that one of these women, Mrs. Charles Cleveland, visited the Women's Pavilion with her husband on October 12th, and then went back again in November at the expense of the WCC-RI to accompany Mrs. Shaw and bring the RI work home. But there are no indications she went down as part of a RI delegation visit.

Certainly, *some* RI women might have visited the Women's Pavilion between the Centennial opening May 10th and the beginning of the Visitors' Register on July 10th. For example, we know that Sarah Doyle visited the World's Fair because she gave a talk on the educational exhibits she saw there to the newly formed RI Women's Club on October 4, 1876.[49] Undoubtedly Doyle would have visited the

[44] Records MS, April 14, 1876 and November 2, 1876.

[45] Records MS, May 19, 1876. On April 14th, the group met to plan and fund Shaw's trip to the Centennial with the RI women's exhibits. The next meeting is one month later, on May 19th, when they summarize the financial situation and adjourn until the fall. They only meet to arrange for someone to collect the exhibits and then they postpone all meetings again, indefinitely.

[46] HSP Manuscript AM3416: Register of Visitors Women's Dept. International Exhibition July 10 – Nov 2, 1876. Donated to the HSP in 1931 by the Germantown Historical Society, probably by Hannah Zell who founded the library there and donated her scrapbooks on the Centennial to the Philadelphia Museum of Art. This large leather volume might be the second volume, or perhaps they just decided to start a visitors' log after it began. The GHS and HSP have no history of a first volume. The Hannah Zell collection is a fairly-complete archive.

[47] 74,000 visitors went to the Exhibition on an average day. (Hannah Zell Scrapbook news clipping: "The Centennial: Women's Day at the Exhibition", November 7, 1876.) This implies that roughly 1 in 50 visitors went to the Women's Pavilion.

[48] These two are Cleveland and Brayton. Mrs. CR. Brayton, Vice Chair of Ward #1, visited on September 19th. The third active member was Mrs. HB Aylsworth, signing on Oct 10; she was a Ward #1 member. Less certain if they are the same person as Centennial members are: Miss Anna Jackson, Ward #9 committee member; Emily Manton, Ward #10 committee member with Mrs. Metcalf, possibly, on Oct 5th; Mrs. Jane E. Fiske, might be Mrs. F. Fiske of Ward #7 (active in the Carnival Authors) who went on Oct 7th; Mrs. W.H. Sheldon might be Mrs. Israel R. Sheldon from the first newspaper committee, who signed the Visitor's Register on Oct 5th.

[49] Secretary's First Record Book of Meetings of the RIWC Jan 16, 1878, RI Woman's Club Archive, Rhode Island Historical Society.

Kindergarten at the Women's Department, and probably, as a member of the original newspaper committee, she would have stopped to see the *New Century* being printed there. So, we might conclude that Doyle is representative of the many Centennial women who visited the Women's Pavilion but didn't sign the Visitors book either because they just didn't, for one reason or another, or because they visited between May 10th and July 10th. Or we might conclude that only a handful of the RI women felt enough of a connection to the Women's Pavilion to visit the interior exhibitions, *and* proudly sign the Visitor's Register.

Is it possible that these affluent women never attended the Centennial? It seems unlikely, especially considering the ease with which the head of the WCC-RI dashed off to Philadelphia in October 1875 to consult with Mrs. Gillespie. Furthermore, after the design school was proposed, "one of the Centennial Committee" penned a newspaper letter to the newspaper editor mentioning that "the art specimens in the Women's Pavilion, from the Cincinnati School of Design, furnish an example for Rhode Island to follow", clearly showing that someone on the committee visited the Pavilion and was inspired.[50] But without other documents, the cautious conclusion might be that few of the RI Centennial women visited the Women's Pavilion. Unlikely as it seems, Helen Rowe Metcalf might *not* have seen the important exhibitions at the Women's Pavilion showcasing design schools for women.[51] More research is needed.

---

[50] *Providence Evening Bulletin*, January 25, 1877, 2.
[51] Eliza Radeke was a hostess. See: Elizabeth Leuthner, "Progressive Women, Egalitarian Ideas," *RISDviews* (Fall 2002), 7.

At the Women's Pavilion: the RI Exhibits in Context

As late as March 1876, with the Centennial opening two months away and 100 square feet of display place assigned to them, the RI women still did not have work collected from RI women to display at the Women's Pavilion.[52] On March 6th, the RI Committee on Women's Work expressed plans to advertise locally for work and make "an appeal for nice work".[53] Someone would be at the Centennial rooms daily from 11-4 to collect the work.[54] We know that about one month later, Mrs. James Shaw, chair of the Women's Work Committee and her Committee secretary, Mrs. Cleveland, had finished gathering the work and the WCC-RI authorized them to travel to the Centennial "as long as necessary to set up and oversee the work".[55]

The RI Centennial women's contribution to the Women's Pavilion is listed in Table 1. on pages 25-6. The categories were given by the Centennial, and are a topic in themselves.[56] A few RI Centennial women did elect to send their own work, and the RI committee collectively contributed a copy of their remarkable newspaper, *Herald of the Centennial*.[57] But the RI group did not rally to interpret "women's work" with the same focus on a woman's right to economic self-sufficiency that so inspired Mrs. Gillespie in promoting an independent Women's Pavilion. The final curated exhibition of work by RI women was more a display of leisure handiwork than a tribute to new employment opportunities for RI women. This same tension ran throughout the Women's Pavilion exhibitions and many critics commented on it. One alluded specifically to the work of RI women: "In this collection of American work we find specimens of tatting-work that rivals the lace. Mrs. John W Hoard of Providence, Miss Daisy Cheney, East Greenwich, RI and [others...] send specimens, .. not done for pay. ... if ladies of leisure would note the time actually spent in making these delicate fabrics women might receive less charity and get paid close to an honest wage".[58]

---

[52] Records MS, March 6, 1877. The building contained 30,000 square feet. See: *McCabe's Illustrated Centennial* (1876), 654. National headquarters allocated the space beginning on February 29, 1876.
[53] Records MS, March 7, 1877.
[54] Records MS, March 6,13 1876.
[55] WCC-RI Minutes, April 14, 1877.
[56] This was the first World's Fair that used a strict system of exhibition categories.
[57] Mrs. James Shaw Jr. appears to be the daughter of the Women's Work Committee Chair. Others include: Mrs. W.H. Reynolds, Ward #8 Chair; Clara Congdon; Miss Daisy Cheney; and possibly Mrs. N.M. Bradley, if she is Mary E. Bradley.
[58] "The House We Live in," *New Century* (June 3, 1876), 25-6.

Clearly, the RI Centennial women did not follow up on their original intention of soliciting only work from "lady artists of merit." In October 1875, their wish list for a RI exhibit consisted of the following artists:

> Lady artists of merit to consider: Mrs. Stridley, Miss Rose Peckham, Miss Coleman, Miss MA Potter, Mrs. Messick, Miss Armington, Mrs. Belcher, Miss McGary, Miss Wheeler, Mrs. Maxfield, Miss Emily Kenyon, Miss Austin, Miss Talbot, Miss Polley.[59]

Only two women from this original list did send work to the Women's Pavilion.[60] Miss Eleanor Talbot exhibited an oil painting, "Children at Play" and Mrs. Messick showcased the ornamental writing she supported herself with. In the advertisements Mrs. Messick took out in the *Herald of the Centennial*, she solicited work for "memorial ribbons for funeral wreaths, crosses, crowns, designed with mottoes, quotations, initials and flowers by … indelible ink marking in every style done to order."[61] Mrs. Messick's ornamental writing is especially important because we know that the RI Centennial women chose to give a framed copy of her ornamental written transcription of the US Declaration of Independence to the RI Historical Society as a memorial commemorating the efforts of the WCC-RI.[62] (This donation was made on March 5, 1877 – the day the RISD trustees first met.[63]) Unfortunately, this example of RI women's work from the Centennial is now lost.[64]

More work is needed to place these proposed artists and the actual contributors within the context of what art and design meant in RI in the 1870s. For example, the painters who exhibited at the Women's Pavilion all went on to participate in the Providence Art Club and not RISD. What should we make of this?

Implicit in the very existence of the Women's Pavilion was the challenging question of whether the women of America had anything worthwhile to exhibit. The original intention in 1873 had been to give the women a limited amount of space in the Main Exhibition Hall for a display of women's work that was of an artistic, literary, or useful character.[65] It has been suggested that John Welsh of the US Centennial Commission Board of Finance might have offered this future opportunity to Gillespie as an incentive to get

---

[59] Records MS, Oct 5, 1875.
[60] For example, active Centennial member Miss Kate Austin apparently elected not to contribute.
[61] *Herald of the Centennial*, 73.
[62] "Decision that the finely written "Declaration of Independence" prepared by Mrs. Messick, as a sample of Women's' work for Philadelphia be presented to the Historical Society as a memorial of the Women's Centennial work in Rhode Island." (Records MS, Feb. 7, 1877).
[63] [Mrs. Messick's Declaration of Independence presented to RIHS] *Providence Evening Bulletin*, Tues March 6, 1877.
[64] "Mrs. Messick Declaration of Independence to RIHS. March 5th, 1877". *RIHS Accessions Book, Vol. 2, 1835-1880.* The 1877 entry is for an MS Copy of the Declaration of Independence, now thought to have been deaccessioned.
[65] Second Annual Report of the WCEC, March 15, 1875 (Philadelphia, 1875), 39.

her help selling stock for the Centennial.[66] By May 1875, the Centennial's existence was guaranteed. In fact, so many exhibitors sought space that annexes were built for most of the buildings. On June 7, 1875 Thomas Cochran of the Centennial Building Committee and AT Goshorn, Director General, met with Mrs. Gillespie and the national Women's Centennial committee in Philadelphia and proposed that the Centennial women "raise $30,000 in free gifts before January 1st to erect a building for themselves."[67] As we have seen, the State Centennial Committees agreed to raise the money, and their fundraising efforts became directed toward achieving this common goal. Some scholars have seen the offer of the Women's Pavilion as an almost-insulting ploy used to rid the small women's exhibition from the now over-subscribed main exhibition halls. But a thesis by Ruth Curran reviews all the primary source material and concludes, as I do, that Cochran and Welsh did make this offer of a separate building devoted to women's work as an opportunity -- and challenge -- for the women of the United States.[68]

One can imagine how thrilled Mrs. Gillespie must have been to have the Women's Department expand from a corner of the Main Hall to an entire building. She lost no time in defining what the Women's Pavilion would represent:

> We desired to give to the mass of women who are laboring by their needle and obtaining only a scanty subsistence, the opportunity to see what women are capable of attaining unto in other and higher branches of industry; and to do this effectually [sic], we felt that these exhibits must find place in a space set apart for them alone. We did not shrink from competition with the works of men, but we sought to show our more timid sisters that some women have outstripped them in the race for useful and remunerative employment, and to encourage these to the perseverance sure to be followed by a larger measure of success.[69]

---

[66] Unpublished Honors Thesis. Ruth E. Curran, "'The City of Sisterly Love'" Women and the 1876 Centennial Exhibition. Department of History, Bryn Mawr. (April 28, 1989). HSP, 11. Under Mrs. Gillespie, the Philadelphia women's committee was incredibly successful selling the stock that many feel assured that the Centennial would even be held. (Maas, Brown, Post). Curran,15 notes with sources on how astonished the men were at the "determination and efficiency of the women's committees".

[67] "Minutes of the Women's Centennial Committee of Phil. [sic] 1875-1877" HSP Manuscript AM 3415. See June 7, 1875.

[68] Curran, 11, 18-20. Curran thinks that the women could have stayed in the Main Hall if they had wanted to. Mrs. Gillespie, in the Third Annual Report of March 1876, 5-6 specifically addressed the rumor that the women had been forced out of the Main Hall and restates that the Women's Pavilion was an opportunity to do such things as invite the involvement of women from all over the world. See also: *Report of the Women's Centennial Committee of the Twenty-Seventh Ward* (Philadelphia: Press of Henry B. Ashmead, 1877). The printed authors at the book's end are Chairman Mrs. Chas. McIlvaine and Sec. Miss Emma C. Stacey." HSP box Wr*.225.

[69] Final Report, 7.

The Women's Pavilion would be "a vital idea, and not a depot for deposit" with the goal of addressing "the practical needs of working women".[70] Its mission would be a woman's economic right to self-sufficiency.[71] The many design school exhibits at the Women's Pavilion should be understood within this context. For example, the skilled women from the Cincinnati School of Design could sell their own carved furniture and earn about $8/day, at a time when most laboring women were earning $1.00 a day, and a seamstress might only bring in $2 a week.[72]

Mrs. Gillespie saw the Women's Pavilion as an epochal opportunity and she solicited every manner of women's work. Dozens of women who had received patents showed their work. These included Martha Costen's three-color pyrotechnic emergency flare that the US Government had bought the rights to for $20,000; Mary Nolan's invention of a "Nolanum" interlocking hollow block that could be used to construct walls; and Elizabeth Stiles expandable desk.[73] There was a large display by the groundbreaking Women's Medical College of Pennsylvania and exhibits of artificial teeth by a female dentist.[74] The Women's Pavilion housed a library containing only books written by women, where visitors could stop and read.

The scope of what Mrs. Gillespie wanted the Centennial women to accomplish did not end here. The national committee sponsored a Kindergarten, published a newspaper that was printed on the premises, wrote a book on the charities conducted by women nationwide[75], and compiled a cookbook.[76] They hired a female engineer to run the building. As noted earlier, a woman oversaw every aspect of this industrial domain.

---

[70]"Woman's Day," *New Century* (Nov. 4, 1876), 200.

[71] See Warner in Post, 171 and Curran. Schlereth reports that women represented 20% of the labor force outside the home in 1876. See: Thomas Schlereth, *Victorian America*, 3-4.

[72] "The Cincinnati School of Design Wood Carving Exhibit", *New Century* (June 10, 1876), 33. The average earning was quoted as $500 for three months work. The income for a seamstress is from Curran: 48; for other women, from: "Employment of Women," *New Century* (Sept. 9, 1876),138.

[73] Anne MacDonald, *Feminine Ingenuity: Women and Invention in America (*1992), 94-101. See also Warner in Post, 164-5.

[74] Warner 169.

[75] Mrs. Franklin compiled the RI list of Charities. The only mention of this is in the WCC-RI Minutes, March 20, 1876. See HSP: "List of Charities Conducted by Women."

[76] RI women never mention contributing to *The National Cookery Book Compiled from Original Recipes, for the Women's Centennial Committees of the International Exhibition of 1876* (Philadelphia, 1876). Mrs. Gillespie proudly held the cookbook up as an example of national coordinated work among Centennial women. RI notes they received a Circular on the cookbook from Gillespie, November 29, 1875. But there is no further mention. I would like to thank Giordana Mecagni for help with the cookbook collection of the Arthur and Elizabeth Schlesinger Library on the History of Women in America, Radcliffe Institute for Advanced Study, Harvard University.

Curran's thesis critiques the skilled labor roles presented at the Women's Pavilion for their emphasis on white, middle-class values. No attempt was made to cross class lines and address the needs of unskilled women working joylessly in factories.[77] The expanding employment opportunities portrayed at the Women's Pavilion included the non-manufacturing fields of medicine, invention, teaching, and the arts; with many design jobs highlighted requiring skilled labor that might even be pursued in a small workshop or even a home.[78] As such, these manufacturing jobs were artisanal and carried with them the aura of self-actualization as well as economic self-sufficiency.[79]

Curran argues that the Women's Pavilion's main message was that even middle-class women and their daughters should be striving for financially independence. She persuasively shows how the experience of the Civil War and the financial uncertainties of industrial capitalism had brought home to all American men and women the conviction that there would be periods in any woman's life when women would need to draw on a marketable skill to be self-supporting.[80] It was a risk wives, mothers, sisters and daughters should plan for. Indeed, Curran claims men and women found it easier to unite around a woman's need for lifelong employable skills, than around the cause of women's suffrage.

---

[77] Curran, 55-84.
[78] Ibid., 55.
[79] Ibid., 56.
[80] Ibid., 72-84.

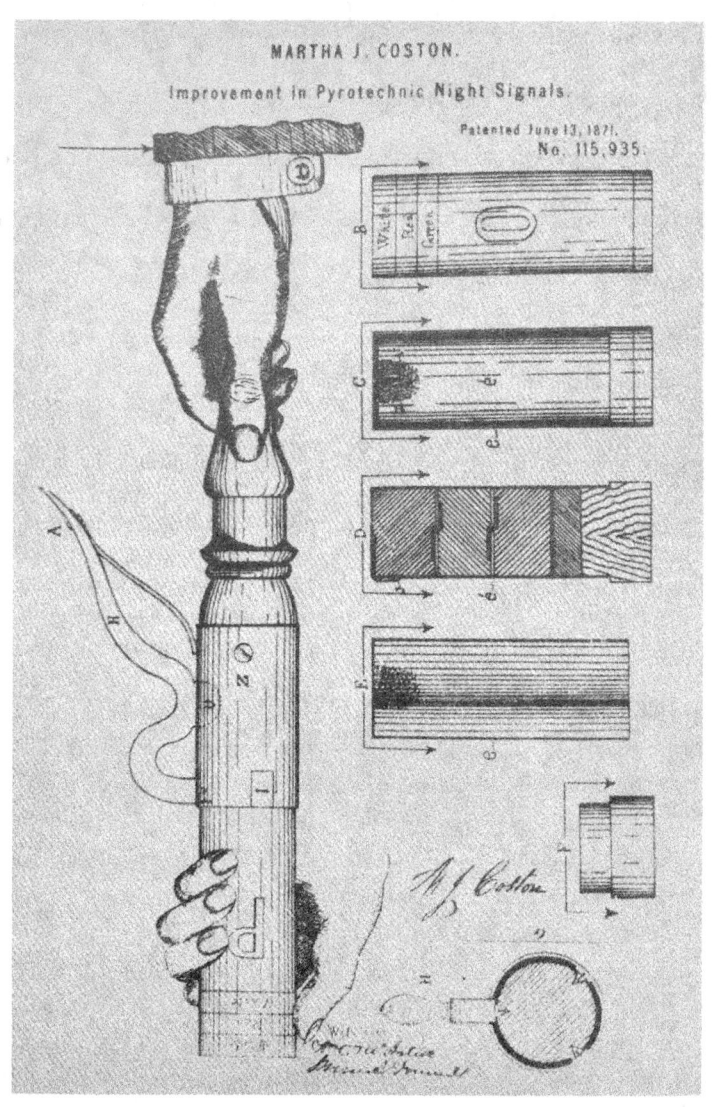

9. Martha Costen exhibited her patented emergency flares at the 1876 Women's Pavilion. Costen sold the rights to her patent to the US government for $20,000.

Table 1.
Work by RI Women in the Women's Pavilion at the 1876 Centennial Exhibition

Sections:
A: Art, Industrial Art, Education   B: Manufacturers, etc.   D: Needlework, Inventions, Patents, etc.
E: Library

No.	Name	City	Entry	Sec.
Woven and Felted Goods of Wool, etc.				
43	Mrs. James A. Wilkinson	Providence	Yarn from the hair of an Esquimaux dog	D
44	Mrs. Edward Bates	Newport	Hand spinning and carding of wool & flax	D
Clothing, Jewelry and Ornaments; Traveling Equipment				
62	Miss Fannie E. Dyer	Providence	Child's Apron	D
64	Miss Mary Jane Gardiner	Warwick	Trimming Cutter	D
72	Employment Society	Providence	a. Infant's shirt, child's skirt and afghan	D
			b. Embroidered flannel skirt	D
74	Mrs. James Shaw, Jr.	Providence	Infant's socks	D
75	Mrs. Sallie O. Summer	Providence	Mittens	D
105	Mrs. Edward Larkum	Providence	Crochet tidy	D
106	Mrs. John H Arnold	Pawtucket	Pincushion cover and tidies in antique lace	D
107	Mrs. N.M. Bradley	Providence	Embroidered suspenders	D
108	Miss Lina Kelley	Providence	Pincushion cover in antique lace	D
111	Mrs. WH Reynolds	Providence	Embroidered flannel shirt	D
116	Miss Florence Ralston	Providence	Tatted tidy	D
117	Mrs. John W. Hoard	Providence	Netted tidy	D
118	Miss C.A. Congdon	Providence	Children's afghans	D
119	Mrs. Andrew J. Carroll	Providence	Netted shawl, afghan, handkerchief	D
120	Mrs Victoria Walker	Providence	Embroidered carriage robe and child's skirt	D
122	Miss Daisy Cheeny	E. Greenwich	Tatted tidy	D
123	Mrs. Abby N. Wiggin	Providence	Button holes in silk	D
124	Mrs. Fanny G Brown	Providence	Embroidered sofa pillow	D
141	Miss E.W. Purkis	Providence	a. Tatting in thread and silk	B
			b. Cross in spatter work	B
142	Mrs John S. Palmer	Providence	a. Tidy and barb in tatting	D
			b. Tidy in spatter work; Cross made from pith of Japan rose	D
171	Miss Julia M. West	Bristol	Cross in spatter work	B

Educational Systems, Methods, and Libraries

| 209 | Women's Centennial Committee | | Volume of Herald of the Centennial | E |

Sculpture

| 242 | N.M. & M.A. Cutler | Providence | Carved wall pocket, glove box, hanging cross, and frame | A |

Painting

349	Miss H.M. Cook	Providence	Painting: Snow Scene	A
352	Miss Kate Paul	Providence	Beethoven and Quartette. Copied in oil from an engraving	A
359	Miss Eleanor W. Talbot	Providence	Oil painting: Children at Play	A
365	Margaret M. Anthony	Providence	Oil Painting: Fruit	A
366	Mrs. Thos E. Studley	Providence	Child's Portrait in Oil	A

Drawings, Photographs

468	Mrs. J.A. Davis	Providence	Marking in indelible ink	A
487	Mrs [John] Messick	Providence	Ornamental Writing:Washington's Farewell Address; Declaration of Independence*	B
508	Miss M.M. Luther	Warren	Painted Photograph: An Interior	A
510	Miss Chapin	Providence	Colored Photograph of Commodore Whipple	A

Ceramic Decorations, Mosaics, etc.

| 528 | Mrs. F.B. Hinds | Providence | Hair wreath | B |
| 549 | Miss H.M. Cook | Providence | Book, with illustrations in birch bark | A |

Hothouses, Conservatories, Graperies

| 582 | Miss Emma Shaw | Elmwood | Pressed ferns | B |
| 583 | Mrs. B.J. Luther | Providence | Mosses from Narragansett Bay | B |

* In 1877, at the close of the Centennial, this work by Mary B. (Currier) Messick (1814-1903) was presented to the RI Historical Society "as a sample of Women's work for Philadelphia … [and] as a memorial of the Women's Centennial work in Rhode Island." At some point, this example of ornamental writing is believed to have been deaccessioned from the RIHS, and is now lost.

November 1876 to January 11, 1877: Design Schools and an Ongoing Sisterhood?

When the world's fair ended in November 1876, so too did the *raison d'être* of the Centennial Women. At both local and national levels, the women turned to addressing two general questions: Would they continue to affiliate in a new organization? How would they use any money remaining in their treasury? The RI women's decision to found RISD is an even more remarkable achievement when considered against the backdrop of how those same questions were answered at the national level. The general assumption has been that Mrs. Gillespie was the fire behind the post-Centennial Philadelphia Museum and newly-founded, companion design school. This implies that RISD's founding developed from a model provided by Mrs. Gillespie and the national committee. A careful attention to chronology reveals that nothing could be further from the truth.

Before the Centennial was half over Mrs. Gillespie went looking for ways to continue the organizational apparatus she had created. As early as September 29, 1876 she addressed the national committee at the Academy of Music and presented her ideas "for a Memorial worthy [of] this organization". Her first thought was to have the Centennial women found a "Music Hall and School" which was "so much needed in this country to refine the tastes of the public and raise art."[81] Music, as we have seen from the episode with the Wagner commission, mattered more to Gillespie than art or design. However, from the very beginning, Gillespie's proposal for founding a Music School met with opposition. Some women thought that a charitable organization like the Red Cross would be better, but other women vetoed this proposal because it did not embrace all creeds.[82] The Ward Chairs met briefly with their constituents and then decided to return at a future date with a vote on what they wanted to support and how to proceed.

By the time the Philadelphia women gathered again on October 13, 1876 the question had changed to this: "whether their organization wished to continue after the close of the Centennial Exhibition, to work together in some National undertaking which should unite them all as heretofore." Each of the Ward Chairs rose and reported on their member's decision. The responses varied from agreeing that most would like to

---

[81] WCC-US Minutes, September 29, 1876. Her interest in music education should not have been a surprise to anyone at this point, but it is curious that Mrs. Gillespie felt confident that the entire organization could be turned to support the cause of music education.
[82] WCC-US Minutes, September 29, 1876.

continue working on "any national object that would be agreed upon", to the adamant statement that the Chair would resign if a Music School was decided upon.[83] No mention was ever made of a Music School again. The women concluded the meeting by passing the resolution: "that the organization of women, now existing, which had for its objects the successful carrying on of the 'Centennial Exhibition', the uniting of the people of our Country, and the advancement of woman through her work be continued and that we invite the cooperation of women in all the states of our union in all the above-named objects."[84]

This invitation must have gone out to all the State Committees, but the RI women make no mention of it in their two meetings that fall.[85] This contrasts to the Boston Centennial women who were enthusiastically involved with the national planning by the end of October, actively participating in the debate over the name. They insisted on the inclusion of the word "National", while other women worried about the connotations of the word "League" and still others felt omitting the word "Centennial" would be like removing a father's name from a child.[86] The Women's Centennial National League (WCNL) was finally founded on November 25, 1876 in the Philadelphia Academy of Music.

However, having set up this national organization, Mrs. Gillespie turned her attention elsewhere and does not seem to have continued with that organization. She had encountered strong opposition at the meeting where the WCNL was founded, and this probably influenced her decision to leave the country for four years.[87] Mrs. Gillespie left for Germany on April 26, 1877 to pursue her daughter's music education and did not return until 1881.[88] Newspaper reports insinuated that Mrs. Gillespie was jockeying to get a position organizing an exhibit of women's work for the upcoming Paris World Fair of 1878. But it is not well known today that the discontent of the US Centennial Women meeting in Philadelphia had risen to such a

---

[83] Ibid., October 13, 1876.
[84] Ibid.
[85] Records MS, November 2 and Dec. 27, 1876.
[86] WCC-US Minutes, Oct. 30, Nov. 6. Also, "Report of Adjourned Meeting of the Women's Centennial Committees" and "The National Centennial League", *New Century* (Nov. 4, 1876), 199,200 and "The Centennial Committee of Women form a League," *Philadelphia Public Record* (Nov. 25, 1876).
[87] The Hannah Zell scrapbook and the Minutes make disparaging remarks about the disruptions caused by Miss Mary Nolan of St. Louis. This is a fascinating story to follow up on. See McDonald, *Women of Invention*, 96ff on the building materials and other inventions exhibited at the Centennial by Nolan. The Zell scrapbook contains other newspaper accounts of this meeting that suggest how strongly opposed some women were to the dictatorial style of Mrs. Gillespie.
[88] Gillespie, *Remembrances*, 331, 371-2.

level that an alternate ballot of candidates had been drawn up and circulated before the vote on who would run the nascent WCNL.[89]

Despite this opposition, Mrs. Gillespie's admirers defended her zealously. By December 6th, her friends began mailing out requests for donations to be given to Mrs. Gillespie now that all the Centennial organizations were wrapping up and she would be out of a job.[90] The Philadelphia Centennial Committee continued to aggressively hold fundraisers whose proceeds would be divided between the Executive Committee and the Wards.[91] On February 2nd the Women's Executive Committee of Philadelphia, with the consent of the Wards, voted to give Mrs. Gillespie all the money left in their budget.[92] The final "testimonial" given to Mrs. Gillespie amounted to $7,800.[93]

Mrs. Gillespie's work on the exhibits at the 1876 Centennial Women's Pavilion and her later involvement with the Philadelphia Museum and School of Industrial Art are understood today as examples of her seamless involvement with art and design. This is not accurate. As we have seen, music was the art form that registered most strongly with Mrs. Gillespie. She allocated over $7000 to music at the Centennial and her first proposal for a memorial to the Centennial Women was for a Music School. After her efforts failed to leverage her position at the WCC into the head of the new organization of the WCNL, Mrs. Gillespie left the country for four years to advance her daughter's music education. It was not until the 1880s that Mrs. Gillespie became actively involved in the affairs of the Museum and School.[94] She was asked in 1883, upon her return, to gather members of her old committee together and help raise funds for the Museum

---

[89] See news clippings in the Hannah Zell Centennial scrapbook, especially: "Centennial league: Lively Scenes at the Academy" and one beginning "It had been smoldering and bubbling for some time..." [Archives, Philadelphia Museum of Art.]

[90] Letter sent out included in the Hannah Zell scrapbook.

[91] The largest was a Calico Tea Party held on February 22, 1877. Planning for this fundraiser began January 5, 1877 with the proceeds to go to "charitable purposes". WCC-US Minutes, Jan. 5,12, Feb. 2, 1877.

[92] WCC-US Feb 2, 1877. *Final Report*, 34. This gift was $3009.34. Not all the Philadelphia Wards turned their fundraising surplus over to the Executive Committee. The 27th Ward thought that the money should be used for charitable purposes within their own ward, since that was where the money had been raised. *Report of the Women's Centennial Committee of the Twenty-Seventh Ward* (Phil: Press of Henry B. Ashmead, 1877) printed authors at end Chairman Mrs. Chas. McIlvaine and Sec. Miss Emma C. Stacey." HSP box Wr*.225.

[93] *Final Report*, Appendix 6, 90.

[94] See for example, Mrs. Gillespie's *Remembrances,* 371-2. Archivist Susan Anderson's October 2002 review of the Philadelphia Museum Board of Trustee Minutes confirms that Mrs. Gillespie's involvement dates to 1883, not the 1870s.

and School.[95] But Mrs. Gillespie never showed any continuous, special commitment to the museum, or to design education, in the 1870s.

Thus, there was no *WCC-US* precedent coming out of Philadelphia for the RI Centennial women to draw on in the winter of 1876-7. The national committee's efforts to establish a Memorial did not extend beyond appointing a Board of Trustees for a Women's Centennial "Memorial Fund" whose goal would be to use the allocated $2155.50 "to be applied (at some future day) towards the erection in this city, of some *useful* Memorial of the work accomplished by the women of America for the proper celebration of the Centennial Anniversary of the establishment of our Government."[96] It is not known whatever happened to this Memorial Fund, but even the resolution to set up this Memorial Fund post-dates the WCC-RI vote to found RISD. This does not mean that the RI women were not inspired by the general planning for the Philadelphia Museum and School of Industrial Art that grew out of the earliest visions for the Centennial, beginning in 1872.[97] Rather, it should be acknowledged that the RI women apparently were setting a unique precedent among US Centennial Women when they voted on January 11, 1877 to use their surplus funds to found a school of design.

Throughout the fall and early winter of 1876-77, the RI Centennial women did not participate in any of the national plans to continue the work of the WCC under the new umbrella of the WCNL. Indeed, the

---

[95] Gillespie, *Remembrances*, 372-3. Gillespie established the Associate Committee of Women at the Philadelphia Museum around this time.

[96] *Final Report*, 16. The Resolution read: "That the Committee on Charities of the Women's Centennial Executive Committee be appointed Trustees of for the 'Memorial Fund,' to which the contributions from all the States represented in the organization (as far as heard from) have been appropriated, except those from the States of New York and Connecticut." This fund also would hold all future revenue from the sale of the national cookbook or Wagner's March, for example, as well as paying any outstanding bills. The RI women did, in fact, release money due them from Philadelphia for the establishment of this Memorial at Philadelphia. At their December 27, 1876 meeting the RI women discuss and then finally agree to allow the national committee to keep their share of the money "realized by the sale of the Women's Building". However, they reserve "the right to vote upon the nature of the memorial." (WCC-RI Minutes, Dec. 27, 1876.) The sale of the Women's Pavilion on December 1, 1876 had generated $1,286.25. (Final Report: 28.)

[97] The US Centennial Commission had planned as early as December 4, 1872 to establish a "Museum of Art and Science Applied to Industry" as an outcome of the Centennial. The scope of this interesting project is described in: "Section 12. "Museum of Art and Science Applied to Industry" (December 4, 1872) "Report to Congress by the US Centennial Commission: A Classified Compilation of the Journal of the proceedings of the Commission and other Papers." Washington: Govt. Printing Office, 1873, 147-152. The Minute Book for the Pennsylvania Museum and School of Industrial Art opens on September 10, 1875, 4. Its stated goal was: "A Museum of Art in all its branches as applied to Industry and in all its technical applications, and to provide in connection therewith, with a special view to the development of the Art Industries of the State of Pennsylvania." The model and inspiration was the South Kensington Museum of London that had grown similarly out of the 1851 Crystal Palace Exhibition. The Museum opened on the anniversary of the Centennial, May 10, 1877 and the school commenced on December 17, 1877. Mrs. Gillespie sailed from Philadelphia on April 26, 1877 and returned in 1881.

WCC-RI had adjourned all activities from May 19th to November 2nd, 1876. The only purpose of their brief November meeting was to authorize two members to travel and collect the RI exhibits; at the end of this meeting they again postponed all meetings indefinitely.[98] However, on December 27th the WCC-RI came back to life to settle outstanding business and disband.[99] They planned to have one final meeting, January 11, 1877 at the house of the Treasurer. At that time, they intended to have a member present a report of the entire work of the WCC-RI.[100] Then they would vote on how to distribute the fundraising money that was still on deposit. There is no hint of what would happen on January 11th. However, the detailed nature of the first proposals unleashed that January day suggest that the women, and maybe even the community, had been thinking hard about the opportunities for the $1500 parked on deposit with the WCC-RI.

January 11, 1877: Founding of RISD

At 11am on Thursday January 11, 1877 forty-seven Centennial women gathered in Mrs. Sackett's house in Providence on the south corner of Pine and Richmond.[101] A light snow had fallen the night before. Some of the women had traveled by carriage from as far away as East Greenwich, but most were from Providence and a few were neighbors.[102] The Executive Committee had placed an announcement of the meeting in the *Providence Journal* on Wednesday and Thursday morning, calling for a "General Meeting of the Women's Centennial Committee of Rhode Island".[103] No one probably had any idea how many women

---

[98] Records MS, Nov. 2, 1876.

[99] They voted unanimously not to incorporate with the Reform Club at this meeting, since "we have never departed from our legitimate way."

[100] This report has never been found.

[101] Architectural historian Mac Woodward has researched the Sackett home once at 168 Pine St, on the southern corner of Richmond. In a May 22, 2002 email to the author, Woodward wrote: "The building, replaced in the early twentieth century, was on the site by 1857, when it appears in the Walling map of Providence. The 1877 directory lists this as the residence of Mrs. Adnah Sackett; the 1882 G.M. Hopkins atlas of Providence indicates that this belonged to the Sackett Estate. The house was still on site in 1908. What intrigues me here, however, is that the building now on the east corner, across the street from number 168, was built in 1896 as an investment by Jesse Metcalf and Gustav Radeke." Nancy Sackett's husband was Adnah Sackett, a jeweler in partnership with Thomas Davis. That is, the husbands of Nancy Sackett and radical feminist Paulina Wright Davis (died August 1876) were business partners.

[102] For example, Eliza Manchester (247 Friendship St), Mrs. Hawes (428 Pine St.), Mrs. ES Jackson, and Sarah Doyle (87 Chestnut St.). But Doyle was a teacher and, like other working woman in the WCC-RI, might not have attended an 11 o'clock meeting. [Note that Sarah Doyle's brother was the Mayor and she became Principal of the Providence Girl's High School around this time.]

[103] *Providence Journal* (January 10, 1877), 2. Repeated January 11, 1877, 2. "A General Meeting of the Women's Centennial Committee of Rhode Island is called for Thursday, Jan. 11, at 11 o'clock, at the house of the Treasurer, Mrs. NP Sackett, corner of Pine and Richmond streets. A full attendance of the Committee is requested. Eliza S. Manchester, Secretary Mrs. FW Goddard, Chairman"

would turn out for this, the supposedly final, meeting. Nancy Sackett's house was not particularly large, probably a side-hall-plan Greek Revival house with a double parlor.[104]

The issue of women and space is a fascinating one, and this meeting at Nancy Sackett's triggers all sorts of questions. Where did all the forty-seven women who showed up sit?[105] What did they do at 11 o'clock? Did they eat lunch? How long did they stay? How did the culture of this space influence their decision-making process? It is noteworthy that once the RISD Board of Trustees is established the meetings take place in downtown office buildings.

Who was at this meeting? It is possible to draw up a list of who definitely attended and who was likely there based on their ongoing involvement in WCC-RI activities. However, these numbers never add up to identifying more than thirty-five or six of the forty-seven women we know were present. The conclusion must be that the final winning vote to found RISD is based on the support of rank and file Ward members who will never be identified. In the end, RISD owes its existence to popular support among anonymous members of the WCC-RI who showed up.

A complete roster of all RI Centennial women participants is included in the Appendix.

Table 2. on the following page is a list of the WCC-RI members who were probably at Nancy Sackett's house on Pine Street in Providence that day.

---

[104] I am indebted to Mack Woodward for his research on this house. See also: Hopkins *1875 Atlas of Providence,* Vol. 2, plate B, p15. [RIHS Graphics] I also would like to thank Dana Munroe at RIHS Graphics for her help in my attempts to locate images of these early landmark locations.
[105] Architectural historian Elizabeth Cromley has written on women and space. In conversation, she mentioned that one diary noted that caterers were often used for these lunches and, surprisingly, the caterers provided folding chairs – even in the 1870s.

Table 2. Who was at Nancy Sackett's on January 11, 1877?

The following 9 women are documented to have been there:

Elizabeth C. Goddard	Executive Committee Chair
Eliza Manchester	Executive Committee Secretary
Nancy Sackett	Executive Committee Treasurer & host (Ward #5)
Lucy Bucklin	former Providence Ward #5 Chair
Mrs. C. Wesley Fields	Providence Ward #5 Committee member
Mrs. James Shaw	Providence Ward #3 Committee member
Lizzie Andrews	Providence Ward #4 Chair
Helen Rowe Metcalf	Providence Ward #10 Chair
Mrs. Thomas W. Chase	East Greenwich Chair

The following 8 women probably were there as Providence Ward Chairs:

Mrs. Charles Matteson	Ward #1 Chair (after Mrs. Gorham resigned, 10-1875)
Mrs. John R. Bartlett	Ward #2 Chair
Mrs. Albert Durfee	Ward #3 Chair
Mrs. ES Jackson	Ward #5 Chair (after Mrs. Bucklin resigned, 10- 1875)
Mrs. Clifton Hall	Ward #6 Chair
Mrs. Ferdinand Smith	Ward #7 Chair (after Miss Minnie Knight resigned, 1875)
Mrs. William H. Reynolds	Ward #8 Chair
Mrs. Lewis T. Downes	Ward #9 Chair

The following 14 RI women had been active in 1876 and might have been there:

Mrs. CR. Brayton	Providence Ward #1 Vice-Chair (after 10-1875)
Miss Kate Austin	Providence Ward #1 Committee member
Mrs. Charles S. Cleveland	Providence Ward #1 Committee member
Mrs. George Wheaton, 2nd	Providence Ward #1 Committee member
Mrs. Cyrus Taft	Providence Ward #2 Committee member
Mrs. Wm von Gottschlack	Providence Ward #2 Committee member
Mrs. Franklin	Providence Ward #4 Committee member
Mrs. Amos Hawes	Providence Ward #5 Committee member
Miss Anna Whitney	Providence Ward #5 Committee member; *Herald* Editor
Mrs. Wm Greene	Providence Ward #6 Committee member
Mrs. Fredrica Dennison	Providence Ward #8 Committee member
Miss R. Pierce	East Greenwich Committee member
Mrs. F. Fiske	Providence Ward #7 Committee member and Pawtucket member
Mrs. Anna Richmond	Providence Active Member, Endowed Athenaeum fountain

It is unlikely, but the following 5 Chairs[106] from other cities might have been there:

Mrs. Henry T. Brown	Cumberland Chair
Mrs. George Harris	East Providence Chair
Mrs. Charles W. Smith	Pawtucket Chair
Mrs. Thomas J. Spencer	Warwick Chair
Mrs. Cyrus Arnold	Woonsocket Chair

---

[106] More research is needed using, for example, diaries, letters, and other personal archival sources.

The following section will go through the events of the January 11th meeting, as they are recorded in the fragile manuscript *Records – Women's Centennial Executive Committee* in the RIHS. Because of the importance of this meeting and the extremely faded state of the handwriting, I have chosen to quote the entire manuscript record.

The meeting opened with the sharing of information sent from Philadelphia: "Meeting of January 11th at Mrs. Sacketts. The meeting opened with the reading of minutes of last meeting. Reading of a letter from Mrs. Gillespie enclosing news-paper paragraphs - of a letter from John Welsh – President of the Board of Finance." [107] The newspaper clipping from Welsh probably had to do with the nationally disappointing news that the Centennial Stock would not be valued until after the Federal government was repaid $1.5 million.[108] The understanding had been that the money was a grant, but now the government considered it a loan to be repaid first, before the stockholders. This had little bearing for the RI women who had never bothered to push the sale of stock, but it was a blow for the Philadelphia Committee which had sold over $4000 of now-worthless stock.[109]

Upon first reading the *Minutes*, I initially had thought that the $1500 left in the WCC-RI budget came from John Welsh's approval for refunding money from the sale of the Women's Pavilion back to Rhode Island, but this is not the case.[110] As we have seen, in May 1876 the WCC-RI had a fundraising surplus of $2588.57 over and above the $3000 they had given for the Women's Pavilion by the end of January 1876.[111] As late as February 1876 they were still raising money.[112]

---

[107] Records MS, Jan. 11, 1877.

[108] This decision was made at the end of the Centennial. The case was appealed in January 1877 and finally decided by the Supreme Court in November 1877 in favor of the government. Stockholders eventually were repaid 23 cents on the dollar. (Maass, 126). Maas reports that governments have seldom succeeded in having World's Fair be profitable. (Maass, 126) Thus, it is even more remarkable that the Women's Department ended with a budget surplus. Unlike the rest of the Exhibition, they had no admission fee and did not receive any government subsidy.

[109] *Final Report*, 31, 33. The Warwick and Coventry Committees sold $450 worth of stock, but RI Centennial women seem to have sold only one other share. However, prominent RI men such as Jesse Metcalf, Thomas Doyle, and Henry Howard seem to have invested heavily in the Centennial Stock. As late as June 1879 they were still petitioning to get their stock redeemed. (Phil. City Archives Box A-1536 "Memorial to the Honorable the Senate and House of Representatives of the United States in Congress, Assembled, commemorated by an Exhibition of the Arts and industries of all Nations, 1876" Phil: Jas. E. Magee & Co., Printers, 1879.) An earlier report stated that as of April 1876, RI had bought $20,372 worth of stock. "Report of the Executive Committee of the US Centennial Commission", Journals & Reports of the United States Centennial Commission, 1872-76 (Phil: May 1876, 66).

[110] See: Nancy Austin, "What a Beginning is Worth," *RISD Views* (Fall 2002): 4-5. In any event, the sale of the Women's Pavilion only generated $1286.25 (*Final Report*, 28).

[111] Records MS, January 10, Feb. 7, 14, May 19, 1876.

[112] This was for the Carnival of Authors. Records MS, Feb. 14, 1876.

Thus, the RI women almost certainly began their deliberation over what to do with the $1500 fundraising surplus in full confidence that they were acting in accordance with national guidelines. They knew that some sort of national Memorial to the Centennial Women was planned, and they had consented to contribute RI's share of the Women's Pavilion sale to that Memorial. As we have seen, they probably had little sense of solidarity with the national cause; perhaps they felt relief at not having sold stock to their constituents, as urged by Mrs. Gillespie.

The WCC-RI Minutes next record six proposals on how to spend the $1500 left in the RI women's treasury. The detailed nature of the first two proposals suggests planning and outside influence. Both proposals are conservative in nature and seek to create a lasting Memorial by placing the money in an interest-bearing trust for one hundred years. Both were voted down. Subsequent commentary uncovered the RI Centennial Women's deep suspicion that a trust could not be relied upon, based on such contemporary local examples as the failure of the Dexter Trust.[113] (Indeed, Helen Rowe Metcalf's son later founded the Rhode Island Foundation in 1916 in part to address legacy-execution concerns such as this.)

The first proposal was sponsored by Mrs. James Shaw, the woman in charge of gathering examples of women's work in RI and the person who traveled to and from the Women's Pavilion. Her name was omitted from the list of RI members in the Final Report, although clearly she was involved until the end.

> Mrs. [James] Shaw of the 3rd ward [Brown is in Ward #1] presented the following Resolutions – in substance
> 1st – That the $1500 remaining in the treasury be paid into the hands of the Corporation of Brown University in trust.
> 2. That it shall be held and invested & reinvested by them as trustees, and suffered to accumulate till the [year] 1976.
> 3. That from and after the year 1976 the fund shall remain forever as a trust fund in their hands as trustees.
> 4. That the income of said trust fund, or so much as may be necessary, shall be appropriated from time to time after the year 1976 to the collegiate education in Brown University – or some other college of such male or female graduates of the public schools of Rhode Island as shall upon examination be found competent for admission – preference to be given to those who shall pass the dept. examination.

---

[113] Dexter died in 1824 leaving what is now the Brown University athletic fields behind Stimson, Arlington, Lloyd and Hope, as a farm for "the accommodation and support of the poor of the town ..and for no other use or purpose whatever." (RIHS Manuscripts finding aid notes.) By 1872 Providence had violated the terms of the Trust when Hope St was widened. After many attempts, the Dexter Asylum land was finally sold in 1956 to Brown University. (RIHS Manuscript notes.)

A motion was made that these resolutions be passed – the motion had seconded – but was finally lost in the ensuing vote.[114]

We might note that Mrs. Shaw's proposal is closest to the original goals stated in the Articles of Association of the Women's Centennial Association of America, as printed in the *Herald of the Centennial* in March 1875.[115] That is: "The immediate work of the Association is to advance the interests of the approaching "Centennial," yet it is not proposed that its influence for good shall end with the close of the Exhibition. It is believed that a permanent Association, ... will be a more fitting Memorial Monument ... Rather than award medals of honor it will give scholarships, direct service useful to winners such as enabling a course of study...."[116] The decision to have Brown University administer the scholarship also seems unexceptional, except for the glaring problem that Brown did not admit women at this time.[117] But Brown was the most important university in the state, and had been the recipient of the 1862 federal "land-grant" Morrill Act. Historian Switzer has noted Brown's interest in these years in making more of a commitment to the fields of Art, Architecture, and Design, but Mrs. Shaw's proposal would not have advanced this cause, since the proposal envisioned a general scholarship program for women and would not even be available for a century.[118]

The second proposal was by the Chair of the East Greenwich Committee, proving that not all the WCC-RI women at the meeting were from Providence. Mrs. Chace proposed placing the money in trust for 100 years, but this time having the wives of RI government officials oversee it:

> Resolution offered by Mrs. Thos. W. Chase. That $1000 be placed in the hands of Trustees to be invested to accumulate for one hundred years, at which time this amount would reach at compound interest the sum of one million dollars – the Trustees to be the wives of our Senators, Representatives, Governors & Judges of the Supreme Court. At the termination of the hundred years the sum to be expended in some substantial memorial to commemorate the RI women of the Centennial. This resolution was also lost by vote.

---

[114] Records MS, Jan 11, 1877.
[115] *Herald*: March 1875 (1.2):14-15.
[116] Ibid.
[117] Brown did not open a woman's college until 1891. Sarah Doyle served on the 1886 committee that worked to finally permit women access to Brown.
[118] Russell Swtizer, "The Configuration of Aesthetics and Capital" (Master's Thesis, University of Rhode Island, 1998), 117-118. Switzer points out the history of Brown's interest in offering classes in art during these years. In 1876, future RISD founding Trustee Reverend C.A.L. Richards delivered at least one of four "Boat Club Lectures" at Brown on "Art and its condition in America". (Citing: Mitchell: *Encyclopedia Brunoniana*, 35).

This might have appealed to Mrs. Matteson, a Ward Chair and the wife of a Supreme Court Justice, and the wives of former Governors, such as Mrs. Henry Howard[119]. In fact, Mrs. Howard was one of the three Centennial women to serve as an original trustee of RISD.[120] However, the proposal was not pursued.

The third proposal for a drinking fountain turned out to be the most important competitor to the idea of founding RISD:

> Miss Andrews moved that the Resolution in regard to a "Drinking Fountain" in Roger Williams Park lapsed over from the last meeting be taken up. Mrs. Bucklin seconded the motion. - a discussion followed and a vote was taken but the motion was lost.[121]

What was the appeal of a drinking fountain? To begin with, it was a memorial that could be accomplished within the budget. If the 100-year Trust proposals were very grand, the idea of a drinking fountain was immediately attainable. It likely was inspired by the decorative fountain outside the Providence Athenaeum on Benefit St – funded by Anna Richmond in 1873 and designed by architects Ware and Van Brunt. (See page 3.) Water fountains also had temperance overtones that the women of the time would have been aware of. Temperance unions, eager to have the crowds drink water instead of alcohol, had sponsored many of the Centennial Exhibition drinking fountains.[122] These were likely compelling rationales behind the popular proposal to commission an architectural drinking fountain for Roger Williams Park - a new urban park being designed in the later 1870s as an oasis for the city's burgeoning West Side population.

The outcome of the fourth proposal shows how strongly the women wanted to a leave an enduring Memorial to their efforts. Their commemorative instincts sought ownership and an enduring expression.

> The resolution in regard to disposal of our remaining money in Charities was also taken up but lost by a large majority.[123]

---

[119] In the 1890s, Judge Matteson framed the terms of the pivotal Jones Bequest lawsuit that led to the RISD Museum.
[120] Catherine Greene Harris Howard was later a RISD trustee from March 1877-October 1878, or possibly 1880. She was the daughter of Gov. Elisha Harris and her husband had been Governor in the 1870s; he also was the RI representative to the Paris Exhibition of 1878.
[121] Records MS, Jan. 11, 1877.
[122] "...the flowing fountain of the Catholic Total Abstinence Union and several of our own will supply pure water, whilst in a more luxurious way, cooled by ice, it will be furnished by the Sons of Temperance, Grand Division of Pennsylvania, under a beautiful booth ...[and] at many convenient points." *Third Annual Report of the Cent. Board of Finance to the Stockholders,* Phil: JB Lippincott & co., April 19, 1876, 4. (Phil. City Archives, Box A-1536) See also Maass: 130.
[123] Records MS, Jan. 11, 1877.

Helen Rowe Metcalf's proposal to found a school of design was the fifth proposal and seems to have been suggested spontaneously, almost out of the blue. We probably will never know what led her to uncharacteristically speak up at this point, but her suggestion crystallized so many dreams of the past, present, and future that in the end it appears with the force of inevitability.

> Resolution offered by Mrs. Jesse Metcalf that the $1500 be appropriated toward the commencement of an "Art School" in Providence – or "School of Design". It was moved and seconded that the resolution be adopted and a standing vote was taken resulting 31 in affirmation – 13 voting negatively.[124]

Imagine it: forty-four women were sitting down, and with Mrs. Metcalf's eleventh-hour proposal to found a design school – well, thirty-one women stood up in affirmation.

Even though Mrs. Metcalf's proposal won by a seventy-percent majority, the women seemed concerned to find a resolution that would please everyone. Indeed, the rest of the meeting was devoted to building a group consensus. There was one final proposal put forward to postpone the decision for five years, but this was not taken seriously. (Later newspaper discussions suggested this proposal for a five-year delay might simply was intended to provide a larger starting endowment for the new design school.) The Centennial Women demonstrated resolve to democratically decide what must have appeared as a conflict between majority and minority wishes of important women in the group. To proceed, the suggestion was made to decide the issue by closed ballot. The *Minutes* for the remainder of the meeting are as follows:

> A proposition that we shall vote by ballot, & so decided. Vote by. The first ballot stood as follows:

> | | |
> |---|---|
> | School of Design | 20 votes |
> | Drinking Fountain | 10 " |
> | Public Library | 9 " |
> | Brown University | 3 |
> | Charity | 3 |
> | Art Gallery & Library | 1 |

> The "School of Design" & the "Drinking Fountain" having the largest number of votes – it was moved and seconded that a second vote by ballot be taken. Here Mrs. Field asked if this vote shall be final & A vote was taken by the committee passing unanimously. The second ballot was then taken with this result for "School of Design".

> 34 in the affirmative –
> 13 in the negative.

---

[124] Ibid.

The chairman asked that the vote be made unanimous – and it was nearly so – but two or three voting negatively by remaining seated.

Next meeting to be held at Mrs. C. Wesley Field's Cor. Chestnut & Cliffords St. Thursday Feb 1st. Meeting adjournd.[125]

Thus, the vote to found RISD was vetted over four rounds of voting. First, as a proposal, 44 women voted in all, with 31 in favor and three opposed. (Or, 70% in favor.) Then, the various options were put to a vote; at this stage, 46 women voted in all, with 20 voting for the design school and 10 for the drinking fountain. (Or, 43% in favor.) This triggered the closed ballot where 47 women cast votes; 34 were in favor of the design school and 13 chose the fountain. (Or, 72% in favor.) Finally, leadership asked for a standing vote in the hopes of achieving a unanimous vote in favor of the design school, and all but two or three stood in favor. (About 94%.) RISD's founding is embedded in a story of female leadership. In their revolt against the directive style of Mrs. Gillespie, the RI Centennial women sought to build leadership by consensus. The women did not adjourn until they had achieved a near-unanimous conclusion at the end of multiple rounds of voting. In a sense, the process was as important as the outcome.

However, nothing in the two year WCC-RI volume of Minutes prepares one for the leadership roles Mrs. Metcalf assumes at RISD in the months and years that followed. It is worth remembering that even she, herself, tried to renounce the decision to found RISD at the next February meeting of the WCC-RI. But the genie was out of the bottle, and the other members would not stopper her back in. It appears almost as Mrs. Metcalf's destiny to *become* a later-life leader to execute this vision. Helen Rowe Metcalf and the founding of RISD is a case study of how an exceptional leader can unexpectedly arise from a normative group. Until January 11, 1877 Mrs. Metcalf was in many ways a representative RI Centennial Women. However, founding RISD offered Helen Rowe Metcalf new responsibilities that she clearly relished.

---

[125] Records MS, Jan. 11, 1877.

My ongoing research argues that Helen Rowe Metcalf's successful leadership at RISD drew upon her pre-marriage entrepreneurship at Rowe & Company - the newspaper, book store, and tea/coffee shop that she and her siblings owned and ran. Located inside the first-floor corner kiosk of the Franklin House public hotel (on the corner of College Hill and North Main Street), this site (and façade) later became RISD's College Building.[126] Helen Rowe Metcalf's children recreated the façade as an homage to their mother's own young beginnings.

10. Helen Rowe Metcalf moved to Providence as a 14-year old orphan, and invested in and helped run her siblings' newspaper, bookstore, and tea/coffee shop until her marriage in 1852. The Rowe children's newspaper was *Rowe's Mirror*, and includes her writing. The Rowe's newspaper associated with progressives, abolitionists, and social radicals, including the media maven behind Spiritualism.

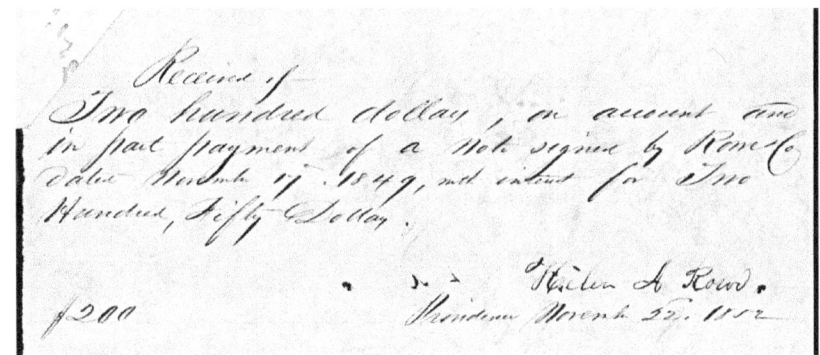

11. The very day Helen Rowe married, the future Mrs. Jesse Metcalf signed this note for repayment from Rowe & Company. "Received of - Two hundred dollars, on account and in part payment of a note signed by Rowe & Co dated November 17, 1849, with interest, for Two Hundred, Fifty Dollars. Helen A. Row $200 Providence, November 22, 1852"

---

[126] Nancy Austin has independently funded and researched Helen Rowe Metcalf's biography in New York State and Rhode Island, and informally presented her research in talks since 2008.

12. Helen Adelia Rowe Metcalf (1830-1895) proposed the idea of a design school to the Centennial Women on January 11, 1877. Her posthumous portrait by Frank W. Benson is now at the Museum of Art, RISD.

The Legacy of the WCC-RI

At the end of a follow-up meeting on February 7th, the women had called for a final meeting to settle all business and present "some plan of action in regard to the appropriation."[127] This "closing meeting of the Women's Centennial Committee" took place on February 22, 1877. Nothing in the record suggests anything resembling a plan of action. There is only one entry for this date and it is concerned to show that the Secretary of the WCC-RI was entrusted to keep the book of Minutes she had maintained these past two years, for as long as she wanted to. At her discretion, she was to present the manuscript to the RI Historical Society "as a proof & remembrance that the several thousand dollars remaining after its work was given to & formed the "nucleus" of the "School of Design" for the city of Providence."[128]

The next installment in this *Ecology of Culture – RI* series establishes how the Trustees of the Women's Centennial Fund were selected. Many came from a proposed Art Association that was being formed to accept the Centennial women's donation. Chaired by ex-Governor Hoppin, over fifty people were involved in this short-lived endeavor, including many artists who later founded the Providence Art Club in 1880. Only three Centennial women went on to become Trustees.[129] One of these women, Catherine Harris Howard, was politically well connected as the daughter and wife of ex-RI governors. However, Harris rarely attended meetings and soon resigned.[130] Thus, only two, very different, Centennial women carried forward: Sarah Doyle and Helen Metcalf. Sarah Doyle was single, a schoolteacher and a staunch feminist who had

---

[127] Records MS, Feb 7, 1877

[128] Records MS, Feb 22, 1877. This final entry was signed by the Secretary, Eliza S. Manchester. Eliza S. Gates presented the volume to the RIHS on February 28, 1902. This gift was noted in the Providence Sunday Journal: Letter to the Editor, "A Foundation Stone," *Providence Journal* (April 13, 1902). The WCC-RI never published a Second, Final Report to follow the detailed record of their enthusiastic First *Annual Report from* January 17, 1876.

[129] These Trustees are identified in the first entry of the RISD Minutes Book: "The Women's Centennial Commission having voted to give the money remaining in their treasury for a school of design, chose the following persons as trustees of the fund for establishment of said school: Rowland Hazard, William B. Weeden, Chas. A.L. Richards, Charles D. Owen, C.B. Farnsworth, Augustus Hoppin, Clifton A. Hall, Francis W. Goddard, Mrs. Jesse Metcalf, Mrs. Henry Howard, Mrs. James M. Drake, Miss Sarah E. Doyle." (Monday March 5, 1877, 1.) It is not clear that either Doyle or Howard were active members, though. Two more Centennial women were represented by their husbands. This includes the husband of the WCC-RI State Chair, Elizabeth C. Goddard. Clifton Hall was an architect of school buildings and remained committed to RISD's success for years. It is not known if Trustee Augustus Hoppin was related to Centennial women Elizabeth, of the 4th Ward in Providence. The fourth female Trustee was Mrs. James H. Drake, apparently of Newport, although possibly a Boston resident who only summered there. Thanks to Douglas Doe, RISD Archives and Bert Lippincott, Newport Historical Society. The Founders Day brochure omits Drake's name from the list of Trustees for March 5, 1877.

[130] I would like to thank Douglas Doe, RISD Archives for sharing with me all of the biographical files he has compiled on RISD Trustees. He has done a formidable amount of legwork in the various archives trying to track down more information on these people.

just established the RI Woman's Club, an important society for clubwomen.[131] Helen Rowe Metcalf was known as the wife of a wealthy industrialist. Interestingly, Helen Rowe Metcalf was finally invited to join Doyle's RI Women's Club the following month, in March, at the same meeting that feminist Elizabeth K. Churchill spoke on "The Industrial Education of Women".[132] There remain many unanswered questions about Helen Rowe Metcalf; it is regrettable that such a dedicated and meticulous record keeper does not have a surviving personal diary in the public domain.

What role did the RI Centennial women play in RISD's history after February 1877? It is well known that Helen Rowe Metcalf was the glue holding the school together from 1877 until her death March 1, 1895 at age sixty, at which point her children take on leadership roles. But what about the other RI Centennial Women? Were they Trustees? Students? Fundraisers? Current preliminary research suggests that few of the women took part in any documented way. However, some played a significant role and these women could form the subject of a future study,

Five RI Centennial women served on the RISD Board of Management, mostly during the 1880s.[133] Ward Chair Harriet Hall's husband, Clifton, served on the RISD Board from 1877-1881, when he was replaced by Nancy Sackett, the former WCC-RI Treasurer. Emma Taft, who might be the formerly active WCC-RI member, Mrs. Cyrus Taft, joined Sackett in her tenure from 1881-1883.[134] Mrs. Charles Matteson, the former 1st Ward Chair who replaced Mrs. Gorham, was on the Board from 1883-84. She was followed by Eleanor Smith, who served from 1885-87, and might be Mrs. Ferdinand Smith, the former Chair of Ward #7. This chronology suggests that the RI Centennial women tried, from 1881 to 1887, to keep at least one former Centennial Woman member on this board, along with Mrs. Metcalf.[135]

Did these women return to RISD as students? Did the women want to set up a Day School they themselves would patronize, or did they see this as more of a charitable endeavor for the working classes,

---

[131] No archival material seems to have survived documenting the remarkable career of Sarah Doyle. For the importance of the RI Woman's Club and clubwomen, see Karen J. Blair, *The Clubwoman as Feminist* (1980).

[132] March 21, 1877 Mrs. Metcalf was presented for membership by Mrs. Morton on March 21, 1877. See [Doyle, Sarah E.] *History: RI Woman's Club 1876-1893. Program of Work for Members. Seventeenth Annual Report March 1, 1893* (1893).

[133] I am indebted to Douglas Doe's compilation of Board of Management members for the cross-listings in this paragraph.

[134] These were the years when the WCC-RI Centennial Endowment Fund was used to keep the school running.

[135] The only other woman to serve on this Board in the nineteenth century was Mrs. Metcalf's daughter, Eliza Radeke. (1886-87; 1890-1931)

or for genteel women who needed to find respectable employment? Unlike other design schools, RISD was unusual in having distinctly different Day and Evening Schools, with distinct curricula. At RISD, the assumption developed that the Day School was for ladies of leisure and the Evening School was for the working classes. In my opinion, this distinction only came about due to the influence of the first Headmaster Charles Barry who was hired July 12, 1878. Barry immediately changed the planned afternoon classes for working women into morning classes that would appeal to a different patron class. He had stressed this position in his long letter of application to RISD and I do not believe RISD would have made this change without his initiative. This is the context for his often-quoted letter:

> We have now considered the school chiefly in a practical and technical sense, that is, in the relation which it bears to the great needs of a manufacturing community; but it is hoped that it will be successful also in interesting ladies and gentlemen of taste and leisure in art studies; for their attendance will increase its power and broaden its influence in another important direction. I hardly need to urge the claims of art as a delightful occupation for leisure hours.[136] [dated on letterhead Boston Art Club 64 Boylston St Boston July 6, 1878]

We know at least some of RISD's Board members hoped to institutionalize this distinction, from the often-quoted letter of William Weeden, the RISD treasurers, dated March 5, 1879:

> We have opened a day school, now in the second term, which numbers some 60 pupils, and an evening school numbering about 80 pupils. The day pupils are generally in independent circumstances, and are being educated for artists, amateurs, and buyers of works of art, and elegant objects. We need a higher standard at large in the community, in order that true design may be appreciated.[137]

Thus, the RI Centennial women appear to have been offered opportunities at RISD when it opened in October 1878. However, the women do not seem to have pursued this opportunity. A newly compiled database on the students who attended RISD's first year Day School shows that eight RI Centennial women, or their children, might have enrolled.[138] Since these pupil's ages range from thirteen to thirty, it could be that the Centennial women's legacy at RISD had more to do with opening opportunity for the next generation, than their own ambition to take classes. The typical RISD student that first year was in their twenties to early thirties.[139] The five most promising people

---

[136] The Barry letter does not end this way. It is one paragraph in a long letter that stresses a more synthetic view of design education. Thus, the idea of a Day School is a more complex issue. See the RISD Archives: Charles Barry 1878 file 3/24 Quoted in Bronson, 9-10 but with introduction and ending omitted.

[137] Bronson,12 notes that the Weeden was trying to get the library funds of the Portsmouth Grove Hospital, which had been collected for benefit of wounded Civil War soldiers.

[138] This is an estimate since many family names, like Jillson, occur on both lists, but from different cities or addresses.

[139] However, there was a thirteen-year old boy, as well as someone in his forties; also, almost forty percent of Day students elected not to give their age.

to research further to determine the overlap between Centennial women and RISD Day students are:

Augusta Brayton

Fredrica Dennison

Louis [sic] Downes

Lyslie M. Hawes

Emily T. Hall

All five, or their mothers, were probably at the meeting to found RISD. It is open to interpretation what these numbers suggest about the RI Centennial Women's intentions in starting a school of design.

On March 5, 1877 nine of the twelve Trustees of the Women's Centennial Commission Fund met at the offices of Mrs. Metcalf's husband. Jesse Metcalf's offices were at Twenty Exchange Place, across from the Tefft-designed train station.[140] A committee was appointed to prepare a constitution and come up with a plan for the organization of a school. The Constitution Committee quickly produced a first draft which envisioned RISD's purpose as follows: "The object of 'The School of Design' is Art Instruction with special reference to Decorative Art and the various practical applications thereof to Industrial pursuits. It shall also provide for Art Exhibitions."[141]

However, the compromise Constitution that was ratified by the Board on April 30' 1877 had the more restrained language of the RISD Act of Incorporation, namely that the goal of RISD "shall be education in Art, with special reference to decorative design." [142] On March 22, 1877 the RI General Assembly had passed the act incorporating RISD with Trustee Claudius Farnsworth's simple statement that RISD was being founded "for the purpose of aiding in the cultivation of the arts of design."[143] At the April 30th meeting where the Board adopted the RISD Constitution, Secretary Sarah Doyle was told to "notify the Women's Centennial Committee that the Treasurer will receive the money to be contributed by them to the RI School

---

[140] Helen Rowe's husband was Jesse Metcalf (1827-1899); their son was Jesse H. Metcalf (1860-1942) – the 1916 founder of the Rhode Island Foundation.

[141] RISD Archives.

[142] RISD Archives.

[143] At this same time, the RI General Assembly released the results of its year-long study on the need for Industrial Arts in RI public schools. The report was written by Newport educator, Henry Fay, who later joined the RISD Board in the its third year. In his report, Fay mentioned plans for the new design school and suggested that its focus might be on the industrial training of girls. (Curiously, I recently discovered Henry Fay is my paternal ancestor. His brother, William W. Fay, came to Newport as an educator when the US Naval Academy relocated from Annapolis to Newport from 1861-65 during the Civil War.)

of Design."[144] On May 16th, the RISD Treasurer received $1675 from Nancy Sackett, Treasurer of the RI Women's Centennial Executive Committee.[145] The next day, RISD opened a bank account with the Hospital Trust Company with an "Endowment Fund" of $1675.[146]

After this flurry of activity and the transfer of funds, nothing happened for a year.[147] In April 1878, the Trustees finally met again and began working to build a viable coalition that would allow the school to open in October 1878, and financially survive the early years. This pragmatic alliance between individuals, businesses, the state, and student tuition is documented in Table 3. In order to keep the school running, the entire RI Centennial Women's Endowment fund was consumed in the fourth and fifth year. Still, somehow, RISD made it through the first twelve years until 1890 when the prospect of winning the $25,000 Albert J. Jones Bequest arrived and set RISD on a different path.

"What a *beginning* is worth." Eliza Manchester believed that there could be no price tag on a dream. The RI Centennial women left *hope* as their legacy, and a belief that the community would come to their aid. They knew it was possible for this small initial investment to grow into a Memorial that was more than stone and mortar, even if they can be questioned for assuming others would make it happen. Few things can survive without the day to day vigilance of practical execution, but where would we be without the expanding optimism to dream of beginnings?

---

[144] RISD Archives. First meeting of the Corporation, 9.
[145] Weeden, Treasurer's Report for 1877, 1878, dated April 15, 1878. RISD Archives.
[146] "Reports of the Treasurers, 1877-1916" See entry for May 1877. RISD Archives; and "A Unique Educational Institution: Rhode Island School of Design One of Our Valued Old Customers," *The Netopian* [n.d., c. 1921], 7-11.
[147] There was no quorum for meetings attempted on May 7,14,21,26 and Sept 27, 1877. No memberships were reported in 1877 or Jan-March 1878. They still needed more money to open. RISD's first history in the circular for the 11th year, 1888-89 states: "The financial depression in the year 1877 prevented any practical steps toward opening a school from being taken before April, 1878.

9. Medal sold by the RI Centennial Women to celebrate
painting, sculpture, and the mechanic arts.

Table 3.

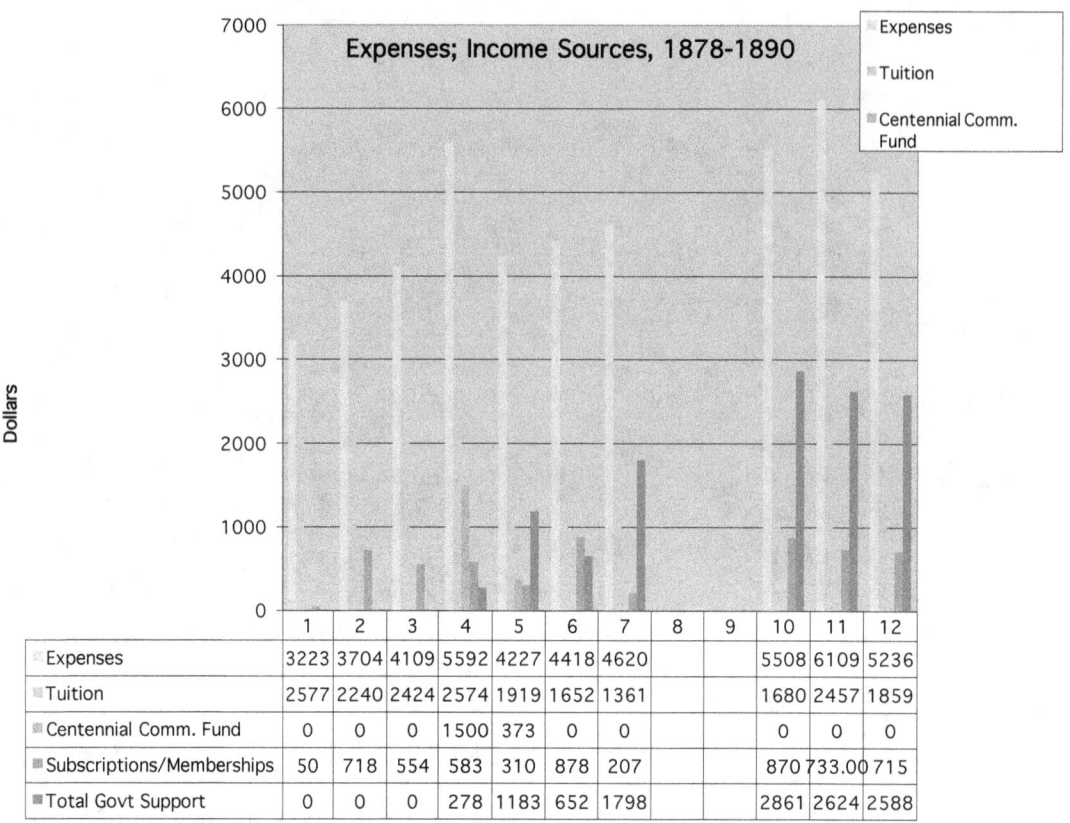

	1	2	3	4	5	6	7	8	9	10	11	12
Expenses	3223	3704	4109	5592	4227	4418	4620			5508	6109	5236
Tuition	2577	2240	2424	2574	1919	1652	1361			1680	2457	1859
Centennial Comm. Fund	0	0	0	1500	373	0	0			0	0	0
Subscriptions/Memberships	50	718	554	583	310	878	207			870	733.00	715
Total Govt Support	0	0	0	278	1183	652	1798			2861	2624	2588

Years (1878-79 to 1889-90)

Table 3. Source Notes:

The data for years 2-7 and 10-12 are from the Reports of the Treasurer at the RISD Archives. There are no records for years 8 or 9. All figures were crosschecked with the 1916 summary document, "Reports of the Treasurers 1877-1916". Year 1: There is no fully-itemized Treasurer's Report for the first school year; however, the report does note ten "initiation" fees of $3 each from the Trustees on April 8, 1878. The 1916 summary document records initiation and member's fees of $49.77, the figure used here. This also is the source for my expense figure of $3223. The first-year tuition figure was calculated from the Registrar's Books for the fall and spring terms: $1292.50 and $1285, respectively. Year 2: the tuition figure does not include receipts from the sewing school ($204.25) or the children's department ($213). Year 3: Again, the tuition figure does not include the sewing school ($167.75) or the Bristol outreach school ($67). Year 4: The tuition figure does not include the Embroidery School ($252.05) or the Bristol-Warren outreach school ($97.67). $1500 of the Centennial Fund is used as income in this fourth school year; it had grown with interest from $1675 to $1872.77 at the end of prior year. The treasurer notes that $372.77 is still on deposit. Years 5-6 are listed on one sheet. It appears that the remainder of the Centennial Fund is used to balance the budget by the end of year 5. In Year 7, Stephen O. Metcalf becomes treasurer and his records are less precise. There are no records for years 8-9. Year 10: the tuition figure does not include the English & Classical School receipts of $100. Under government support I have included the receipts listed for State Fund and State Beneficiaries, as well as the City receipts for both 1886-7 ($349) and 1887-8 ($980). Both sums are recorded as income in 1887-8, perhaps when it was received. I am assuming the records for Year 11, 1888-89 are those posted as the Report of the Treasurer for September 1889, before the beginning of the next school year in October; these are the figures used by the 1916 summary document. In this year, the list of (male) major donors is given; this includes four contributions of $100 each from Henry Steere, C.D. Owen, Jesse Metcalf, and the Brown & Sharpe Mfg. Co. In Year 12, I included into the Subscriptions total the $100 listed separately from Goff, Rice & Smith and the $100 in subscriptions for prizes. This year is not included in the "Treasurers Summary Report, 1877-1916". Throughout the chart, numbers were rounded to the nearest dollar. Expense totals do not include the amount listed on the Treasurer's Reports as being "on deposit", to balance the budget.

Appendix: RI Centennial Women
an alphabetical list of the 280 known participants
by Nancy A. Austin (2002)

Name: RI Centennial Women	Role	First Meeting	Final Report	Founding RISD: 11 Jan 1877
Adams, Miss S.A.	Pawtucket Committee member	no	yes	
Aldrich, Miss E.	Woonsocket Committee member	no	yes	
Aldrich, Mrs. C.E.	Providence Ward Committee member		yes	
Allen, Mrs. B. [J.L.]	Warwick Committee member; Secretary	no	yes	
Amington, Miss C.	Woonsocket Committee member	no	yes	
Andrews, Miss Elizabeth E. (Lizzie)	Providence Ward #4 Chair	yes	yes	Drinking Fountain - proposed
Andrews, Mrs. H.	Providence Ward Committee member		yes	
Andrews, Mrs. W.H.	Providence Ward Committee member		yes	
Anfelt, Mrs. E.	Providence Ward Committee member		yes	
Angell, Mrs Edwin	Providence Ward #1 Committee	yes	no	
Anthony, Mrs. E.	Pawtucket Committee member	no	yes	
Anthony, Mrs. F.	Pawtucket Committee member	no	yes	
Arnold, Mrs.	E. Providence Committee member	no	yes	
Arnold, Mrs. Cyrus	Woonsocket Chair	yes	yes	possible as Woonsocket Chair
Arnold, Mrs. Dr.	East Greenwich Committee member	no	yes	
Arnold, Mrs. G.B.	Cumberland Chair	yes	yes	
Arnold, Mrs. J.Q.	Warwick Committee member	no	yes	
Aspinwall, Mrs.	E. Providence Committee member	no	yes	
Austin, Miss Kate (Katherine)	Providence Ward #1 Committee member	yes	yes	likely, active member
Aylesworth, Mrs. H.B.	Providence Ward #1 Committee member	yes	yes	
Bacon, Mrs. M.S.	Pawtucket Committee member	no	yes	
Balcolm, Mrs. J.C.	Woonsocket Committee member	no	yes	
Ballou, Mrs. H.L.	East Greenwich Committee member	no	yes	
Barker, Mrs. F.A.	Pawtucket Committee member	no	yes	
Barney, Miss E.K.	Warwick Committee member	no	yes	
Bartlett, Mrs. Harvey S.	Warwick Committee member; Treasurer	no	yes	
Bartlett, Mrs John R.	Providence Ward #2 Chair	yes	yes	likely as Ward Chair
Blakeslee, Mrs.	East Greenwich Committee member	no	yes	
Blodgett, Miss ?	Woonsocket Committee member	no	yes	
Blodgett, Miss M.	Woonsocket Committee member	no	yes	
Blodgett, Miss S.	Pawtucket Committee member	no	yes	
Booth, Miss L.	Warwick Committee member	no	yes	
Bosworth, Mrs. W.H.	Pawtucket Committee member	no	yes	
Boulett, Mrs. N	Woonsocket Committee member	no	yes	
Bowler, Mrs. S.	Warwick Committee member	no	yes	
Boyden, Mrs. A.O.	Providence Ward Committee member		yes	
Bradley, Mrs.	Providence Ward #5 Committee member	yes	no	
Bradley, Mrs. Judge C.S. [died]	State Board - original secretary	yes	no, dead	
Brayton, Mrs. C.R.	Providence Ward #1 Committee member; Vice Chair of Ward #1	yes	yes	likely, active member
Briggs, Mrs. B.	Pawtucket Committee member	no	yes	
Briggs, Mrs. Charles	Providence Ward #9 Committee member	yes	yes	
Briggs, Mrs. H.	Pawtucket Committee member	no	yes	
Brown[e], Miss E.	Providence Ward #9 Committee member	yes	yes	
Brown, Mrs.	East Greenwich Committee member	no	yes	

Appendix: RI Centennial Women
an alphabetical list of the 280 known participants
by Nancy A. Austin (2002)

Name: RI Centennial Women	Role	First Meeting	Final Report	Founding RISD: 11 Jan 1877
Browne, Miss F.	East Greenwich Committee member	no	yes	
Browne, Mrs. George H.	Providence Ward #2 Committee member	yes	yes	
Browne, Mrs. Henry T.	Cumberland Chair	yes	yes	possible as Cumberland Chair
Browne, Mrs. Reginald	Providence Ward #5 Committee member	yes	no	
Browne, Mrs. S.H.	Woonsocket Committee member	no	yes	
Bryant, Miss Fanny	Providence Ward #2 Committee member	yes	no	
Bryant, Mrs.	Providence Ward #2 Committee member	yes	no	
Buckley, Mrs. J.	Pawtucket Committee member	no	yes	
Bucklin, Miss Lorraine	Providence Ward #5 Committee member	yes	no	
Bucklin, Mrs. James C. (Lucy Dailey)	Providence Ward #5 Chair - resigned as Chair, 10-1875	yes	yes	Drinking Fountain - seconded
Bults, Mrs. J.W.	E. Providence Committee member	no	yes	
Burgess, Miss Dora	Providence Ward #9 Committee member	yes	yes	
Burnside, Mrs A.E.	Providence Ward #2 Committee member	yes	no	
Campbell, Mrs.	Providence Ward #2 Committee member	yes	yes	
Carpenter, Miss Annie	Providence Ward #3 Committee member	yes	yes	
Carpenter, Miss M.	Providence Ward Committee member		yes	
Carpenter, Miss N.F.	Providence Ward #1 Committee	yes	no	
Carpenter, Mrs. A.	Warwick Committee member	no	yes	
Carr, Mrs. Dr. [Geo.?]	Providence Ward #8 Committee member	no	no	
Caswell, Mrs. Alexis	Providence Ward #2 Committee member	yes	no	
Cavrique, Mrs. R.	Pawtucket Committee member	no	yes	
Chaffee, Miss A.	E. Providence Committee member	no	yes	
Chase, Mrs. Jason E.	Providence Ward #5 Committee member	yes	no	
Chase, Mrs. Thomas W.	East Greenwich Chair	yes	yes	100yr Govt. Trust - proposed
Cheeseborough, Miss	E. Providence Committee member	no	yes	
Cheney, Miss Daisy	East Greenwich Committee member	no	yes	
Claflin, Mrs. George S.	Providence Ward #1 Committee member	yes	yes	
Clapp, Miss M.	Pawtucket Committee member	no	yes	
Clark, Mrs. S.W.	Pawtucket Committee member	no	yes	
Clarke, Miss M.	Pawtucket Committee member	no	yes	
Cleveland, Mrs. Charles S.	Providence Ward #1 Committee member	yes	no	likely, active member
Cole, Miss H.	Providence Ward #9 Committee member	yes	yes	
Cole, Mrs. J.	Providence Ward Committee member		yes	
Conaut, Mrs. H.	Pawtucket Committee member	no	yes	
Congdon, Miss Clara	Providence Ward #1 Committee member	yes	yes	
Cook, Mrs. J.B. (Edward)	Providence Ward #1 Committee member	yes	yes	
Cornell, Miss I.	Pawtucket Committee member	no	yes	
Cummings, Miss	E. Providence Committee member	no	yes	
Curtis, Miss. L.	Woonsocket Committee member	no	yes	
Cushman, Mrs. G.	Pawtucket Committee member	no	yes	
Darling, Mrs. L.B.	Pawtucket Committee member	no	yes	
Dedrick, Mrs. Dr.	Warwick Committee member	no	yes	
Delaney, Miss A.	Pawtucket Committee member	no	yes	
Dennison, Mrs. Fredrica	Providence Ward #8 Committee member	yes	yes	likely, active member

Appendix: RI Centennial Women
an alphabetical list of the 280 known participants
by Nancy A. Austin (2002)

Name: RI Centennial Women	Role	First Meeting	Final Report	Founding RISD: 11 Jan 1877
Dexter, Miss A.	E. Providence Committee member	no	yes	
Dexter, Mrs. H.B.	Pawtucket Committee member	no	yes	
Dexter, Mrs. J.W.	E. Providence Committee member	no	yes	
Donahue, Mrs. C.	Woonsocket Committee member	no	yes	
Downes, Mrs. Dr. W.C.	Providence Ward #9 Committee member	yes	yes	
Downes, Mrs. Lewis T. [Final Report: Mrs	Providence Ward #9 Chair	yes	yes	likely as Ward Chair
Doyle, Miss Sarah	Providence Ward #5 Committee member	no	no	
Dudley, Mrs. Thos.	Providence Ward #3 Committee member	yes	no	
Durfee, Mrs. Albert	Providence Ward #3 Chair	yes	yes	likely as Ward Chair
Earle, Mrs. J.D.	Pawtucket Committee member	no	yes	
Earle, Mrs. T.	Pawtucket Committee member	no	yes	
Easton, Miss A.	Pawtucket Committee member	no	yes	
Eddy, Miss F.	East Greenwich Committee member	no	yes	
Edwards, Mrs. Dr.	Providence Ward Committee member		yes	
Eldredge, Mrs. E.	East Greenwich Committee member	no	yes	
Euel, Mrs. A.J.	Providence Ward Committee member		yes	
Evans, Miss Katie	Providence Ward #1 Committee member	yes	yes	
Everett, Mrs.	E. Providence Committee member	no	yes	
Faxon, Mrs. E.G.	Woonsocket Committee member	no	yes	
Fermer [?], Mrs. Herbert	Providence Ward #8 Committee member	yes	no	
Fessenden, Mrs. R.	Pawtucket Committee member	no	yes	
Fields, Mrs C. Wesley	Providence Ward #5 Committee member	yes	no	documented as present
Fifield, Miss S.	Warwick Committee member	no	yes	
Fiske, Mrs. F.	Prov. Ward #7 at inital meeting and Authors 2-76.Pawtucket	no/yes?	yes	possible, active member
Flagg, Mrs. L.	Pawtucket Committee member	no	yes	
Foner?, Mrs Jas. H.	Providence Ward #5 Committee member	yes	no	
Foss, Mrs. S.S.	Providence Ward Committee member		yes	
Franklin, Mrs.	Providence Ward #4 Committee member	yes	no	possible, wrote Charity Report
Gammell, Miss Hope	Providence Ward #2 Committee member	yes	no	
Goddard, Mrs. Frank W. (Elizabeth C.)	State Board - Chair for RI	yes	yes	State Chair, present
Goff, Mrs. C.	Warwick Committee member	no	yes	
Gorham, Mrs. John	Providence Ward #1 Chair - resigned Sept. 21,1875	yes	yes, but had	
Gottschlack, Mrs. Wm von	Providence Ward #2 Committee member			possible, active member
Gould, Miss A.	Warwick Committee member	no	yes	
Greene, Miss L.	Warwick Committee member	no	yes	
Greene, Mrs. Christopher	Warwick Committee member; Secretary	no	yes	
Greene, Mrs. H.L.	Warwick Committee member	no	yes	
Greene, Mrs. L.	Warwick Committee member	no	yes	
Greene, Mrs. Wm	Providence Ward #6 Committee member	yes	no	likely, active member
Griswold, Mrs. Wm.	Providence Ward #1 Committee member	yes	yes	
Hall, Mrs. Clifton	Providence Ward #6 Chair	yes	yes	likely as Ward Chair
Hall, Mrs. Geo. W.	Providence Ward #3 Committee member	yes	no	
Harris, Miss	East Greenwich Committee member	no	yes	
Harris, Miss Alice	Providence Ward #1 Committee member	yes	yes	

Appendix: RI Centennial Women
an alphabetical list of the 280 known participants
by Nancy A. Austin (2002)

Name: RI Centennial Women	Role	First Meeting	Final Report	Founding RISD: 11 Jan 1877
Harris, Miss Sophie	Providence Ward #1 Committee member	yes	yes	
Harris, Mrs. George	E. Providence Chair	no	yes	possible as E. Prov. Chair
Hart, Mrs. Charles	Providence Ward #2 Committee member	no	no	
Hastings, Mrs.	East Greenwich Committee member	no	yes	
Hawes, Mrs. Dr. Amos	Providence Ward #5 Committee member	no	no	
Hazard, Mrs. A.J.	Woonsocket Committee member	no	yes	
Hazard, Mrs. Jeffrey	Providence Ward #4 Committee member	yes	no	
Hill, Miss V.	Pawtucket Committee member	no	yes	
Hilton, Mrs. Wm. D.	Providence Ward #7 Committee member	yes	no	
Hoffman, Mrs. Edward	Providence Ward #2 Committee member	yes	yes	
Holden, Miss	East Greenwich Committee member	no	yes	
Hood, Miss	Providence Ward #3 Committee member	yes	no	
Hoppin, Miss Elizabeth	Providence Ward #4 Committee member	no	no	
Houland, Miss	Providence Ward #3 Committee member	yes	yes	
Howard, Miss	E. Providence Committee member	no	yes	
Howard, Miss N.	E. Providence Committee member	no	yes	
Howard, Mrs. Gov. Henry	Warwick Committee member; Treasurer	no	yes	
Howard, Mrs. H.	Pawtucket Committee member	no	yes	
Howland, Miss M.	East Greenwich Committee member	no	yes	
Howland, Miss S.	East Greenwich Committee member	no	yes	
Howland, Mrs. R.	Warwick Committee member	no	yes	
Hoxie, Mrs.	Providence Ward #5 Committee member	yes	no	
Hulbard, Mrs. A.E.	Pawtucket Committee member	no	yes	
Jackson, Miss Anna	Providence Ward #9 Committee member	yes	yes	
Jackson, Mrs. E.S.	Providence Ward #5 Chair - replaced Mrs. J.C. Bucklin	yes	yes	likely as Ward Chair
Jarches, Mrs. A.	Pawtucket Committee member	no	yes	
Jenches?, Mrs. L.D.	Providence Ward Committee member		yes	
Jenckes, Mrs. E.H.	Pawtucket Committee member	no	yes	
Jerauld, Mrs.	Woonsocket Committee member;FP/ 1-3-1876 Chair of E. Prov.	no	yes	
Jermigan, Mrs.	Woonsocket Committee member	no	yes	
Jillson, Mrs. D.	Pawtucket Committee member	no	yes	
Johnson, Miss L.	Pawtucket Committee member	no	yes	
Kendrick, Mrs. John	Providence Ward #8 Committee member	yes	no	
Kent, Miss M.	Woonsocket Committee member	no	yes	
Kilton, Miss A.	Pawtucket Committee member	no	yes	
Kilton, Mrs.	Providence Ward #3 Committee member	yes	no	
Kimball, Mrs. Herbert	Providence Ward #6 Committee member	yes	no	
King, Mrs. Chas. G.	Providence Ward #2 Committee member	yes	no	
King, Mrs. Fred. K.	Providence Ward #2 Committee member	yes	no	
Kingsbury, Miss G.	Warwick Committee member	no	yes	
Knight, Miss Alice	Providence Ward #6 Committee member	no	no	
Knight, Miss Carrie	Providence Ward #4 Committee member	yes	no	
Knight, Miss Minnie	Providence Ward #7 Chair; retired as Chair late 1875; replaced	yes	yes	
Knight, Mrs. Dr.	Providence Ward #7 Committee member	yes	no	

Appendix: RI Centennial Women
an alphabetical list of the 280 known participants
by Nancy A. Austin (2002)

Name: RI Centennial Women	Role	First Meeting	Final Report	Founding RISD: 11 Jan 1877
Lamphear, Mrs. T.	Warwick Committee member	no	yes	
Lawton, Miss Ella	Providence Ward #1 Committee member	yes	yes	
Leonard, Miss N.	Pawtucket Committee member	no	yes	
Lilley, Mrs. Robt.	Providence Ward #4 Committee member	yes	no	
Lincoln, Mrs.	Providence Ward #6 Committee member	yes	no	
Lincoln, Mrs. George [Mrs. Gov. in Final	Providence Ward #2 Committee member	yes	yes	
Lippitt, Miss J.	Warwick Committee member	no	yes	
Lippitt, Mrs. J.	Warwick Committee member	no	yes	
Littlefield, Mrs. A.H.	Pawtucket Committee member	no	yes	
Littlefield, Mrs. G.L.	Pawtucket Committee member	no	yes	
Luen, Mrs. W.	Warwick Committee member	no	yes	
Lyon, Mrs. Emory	Providence Ward #3 Committee member	no	no	
Manchester, Eliza (Mrs. J.S.) [later Gates]	State Board - Secretary	yes	yes	State Secretary, present
Mann, Mrs. A.A.	Pawtucket Committee member	no	yes	
Manton, Miss	Providence Ward #10 Committee member	yes	yes	
Martin, Mrs. Benjamin	Warwick Committee member	no	yes	
Mason, Miss E.	Pawtucket Committee member	no	yes	
Matteson, Mrs. Charles	Providence Ward #1 Chair after Oct 1875 - after Mrs. Gorham	yes	yes	likely as Ward Chair
Matthewson, Miss A.	Pawtucket Committee member	no	yes	
McCartney, Miss M.J.	Pawtucket Committee member	no	yes	
McGary, Miss M.E.	Providence Ward #7 Committee member	no	no	
Merriweather, Miss	Providence Ward #2 Committee member	yes	yes	
Metcalf, Helen Adelia Rowe (Mrs. Jesse)	Providence Ward #10 Chair	yes	yes	proposed RISD
Metcalf, Miss C.	Pawtucket Committee member	no	yes	
Metcalf, Miss (Sophie?)	Providence Ward #10 Committee member	yes	yes	
Metcalf, Mrs. M.B.	Pawtucket Committee member	no	yes	
Miles, Miss L.	Woonsocket Committee member	no	yes	
Neliman?, Miss	Providence Ward #7 Committee member	yes	no	
Nicholson, Mrs. W.T.	Providence Ward #1 Committee member	yes	yes	
Nislet, Mrs. J.	Pawtucket Committee member	no	yes	
Norton, Mrs.	Providence Ward #10 Committee member	yes	yes	
Owen, Miss	Providence Ward #10 Committee member	yes	yes	
Paine, Mrs. Dr.	East Greenwich Committee member	no	yes	
Patteson, Miss M.	Pawtucket Committee member	no	yes	
Persons, Mrs. B.W.	Providence Ward #3 Committee member	yes	no	
Phettleplace, Miss	Providence Ward #1 Committee member	yes	yes	
Phillips, Mrs. Theodore	Providence Ward #3 Committee member	yes	no	
Pierce, Miss R.[Rohnson?]	East Greenwich Committee member:FP/IstWard Prov. 1-18-1875	no/yes?	yes	likely, active member
Pomeroy, Mrs. E.G.	Providence Ward #5 Committee member	yes	no	
Potter, Miss E.	East Greenwich Committee member	no	yes	
Potter, Mrs. A.	East Greenwich Committee member	no	yes	
Potter, Mrs. Dr. H.A.	Providence Ward Committee member		yes	
Randall, Mrs. C.H.	Pawtucket Committee member	no	yes	
Randolph, Miss	Providence Ward #1 Committee member	yes	yes	

Appendix: RI Centennial Women
an alphabetical list of the 280 known participants
by Nancy A. Austin (2002)

Name: RI Centennial Women	Role	First Meeting	Final Report	Founding RISD: 11 Jan 1877
Rawson, Miss	Providence Ward #7 Committee member	yes	no	
Rawson, Mrs. Rich.	Providence Ward #7 Committee member	yes	no	
Ray, Mrs. S.H.	Woonsocket Committee member	no	yes	
Raymond, Mrs. Benjamin	East Greenwich Chair	no	yes	
Reynolds, Mrs. Wm H.	Providence Ward #8 Chair	yes	yes	likely as Ward Chair
Rhodes, Mrs.	East Greenwich Committee member	no	yes	
Richardson, Mrs. Henry	E. Providence Chair, 1875	no	no	
Richmond, Miss Caroline	Providence Ward #2 Committee member	yes	no	
Richmond, Mrs. Anna (George)	Providence Ward #9 Committee member	yes	yes	Likely – endowed Athenaeum drinking fountain, 1873.
Richmond, Mrs. Howard	Providence Ward #2 Committee member	yes	yes	
Robbins, Mrs.	Providence Ward Committee member		yes	
Robinson, Miss E.	Woonsocket Committee member	no	yes	
Sackett, Nancy (Mrs. Adnah)	State Board - Treasurer	yes	yes	State Treasurer, host, present
Sanders, Miss MA	Pawtucket Committee member	no	yes	
Sawyer, Miss	Providence Ward #3 Committee member	yes	yes	
Schulaith, Mrs.	Providence Ward #1 Committee member	yes	yes	
Seegrens, Mrs. G.E.	Providence Ward Committee member		yes	
Shaw, Mrs. James	Providence Ward #3 Cortlmittee member	yes	no	100yr Brown Trust – proposed
Sheldon, Mrs. Israel R.	Providence Ward #5 Committee member	no	no	
Skinner, Mrs.	Providence Ward #4 Committee member	yes	no	
Slocum, Miss B.	Woonsocket Committee member	no	yes	
Slocum, Mrs. John Slocum	Providence Ward #8;#9 Ward Committee member	yes	no	
Smith, Miss Alice	Pawtucket Committee member	no	yes	
Smith, Miss L	Woonsocket Committee member	no	lyes	
Smith, Miss Stella	Pawtucket Committee member	no	yes	
Smith, Mrs. Charles W.	Pawtucket Chair	no	yes	possible as Pawtucket Chair
Smith, Mrs. E.S.	Woonsocket Committee member	no	yes	
Smith, Mrs. Ferdinand	Providence Ward #7 Committee member; Ward #7 Chair after	yes	no	likely as Ward Chair
Smith, Mrs. M.F.	Woonsocket Committee member	no	yes	
Snow, Mrs. George	Providence Ward #8 Committee member	yes	no	
Spaulding, Miss C.	Warwick Committee member	no		
Spencer, Mrs. Thos. J.	Warwick Chair; organized late,Jan 3, 1876 Minutes	no	s	possible as Warwick Chair
Sprague, Mrs. Dr.	Warwick Committee member	no	yes	
Stafford, Mrs. M.C.	Pawtucket Committee member	no	yes	
Stanley, Miss C.	East Greenwich Committee member	no	yes	
Starkweather, Mrs. J.G.	Pawtucket Committee member	no	yes	
Taft, Mrs. Cyrus	Providence Ward #2 Committee member	yes	no	likely, active member
Talcott, Mrs.	Providence Ward #3 Committee member	yes	no	
Terry, Mrs. AT.	Woonsocket Committee member	no	yes	
Thetcher, Mrs.	E. Providence Committee member	no	yes	
Thompson, Miss LE.	Pawtucket Committee member	no	yes	
Tillinghast, Miss N.	East Greenwich Committee member	no	yes	
Truman, Miss H.	Pawtucket Committee member	no	yes	
Tucker, Miss	Providence Ward #3 Committee member	yes	no	

Appendix: RI Centennial Women
an alphabetical list of the 280 known participants
by Nancy A. Austin (2002)

Name: RI Centennial Women	Role	First Meeting	Final Report	Founding RISD: 11 Jan 1877
van Dyck, Mrs.	Providence Ward #5 Committee member	yes	no	
Walker, Mrs. M.R.	Pawtucket Committee member	no	yes	
Ward, Mrs. C.D.	Pawtucket Committee member	no	yes	
Warland, Mrs. C.	Pawtucket Committee member	no	yes	
Wheaton, Mrs. Dr. J.L. (Marie?)	Pawtucket Committee member:FP/Prov. Ward #6 inital meeting	no/yes?	yes	
Wheaton, Mrs. George (2nd)	Providence Ward #1 Committee member	yes	yes	likely, active member
Whitaker, Miss Ellen	Providence Ward #2 Committee member	yes	yes	
Whitcomb, Miss	E. Providence Committee member	no	yes	
Whiteman, Mrs. Ang	Providence Ward #5 Committee member	yes	no	
Whitney, Miss Anna	Providence Ward #5 Committee member	yes	no	maybe, former *Herald* editor
Whitney, Miss M.	Pawtucket Committee member	no	yes	
Wilcox, Mrs.	Providence Ward Chair	yes	yes	
Wilmaith?, Mrs.	Providence Ward #6 Committee member	yes	no	
Wilson, Mrs. B.	E. Providence Committee member	no	yes	
Wood, Miss A.	Pawtucket Committee member	no	yes	
Wood, Mrs. C.	Pawtucket Committee member	no	yes	

BIBLIOGRAPHY

Archives: Historical Society of Pennsylvania Archives; Institutional Archives, Brown University; John Hay Library Archives, Brown University; Library Company of Philadelphia Archives; Philadelphia City Archives; Philadelphia Museum of Art Archives; Providence Athenaeum Archives; Providence City Archives; Rhode Island Historical Society Archives; Rhode Island School of Design Archives; Rhode Island State Judicial Archives, Schlesinger Library on the History of Women in America Archives, Harvard University.

Period Newspapers: *Herald of the Centennial, New Century for Women, New York Times, New York Tribune, Providence Evening Bulletin, Providence Journal.*

Primary and Secondary Books and Articles:
Academies of Art between the Renaissance and Romanticism (1989).

Allen, Ann Taylor. "Let us Live for our Children: Kindergarten Movements in Germany and the United States, 1840-1914," *History of Education Quarterly* 28 (Spring 1988), 22-48.

Austin, Nancy. "Educating American Designers for Industry, 1853-1903." In *The Cultivation of American Artists: Education and the Commerce of Art in 19th-century America*, ed. Diana Korzenik. (1997),187-206.

Austin, Nancy. "What a Beginning is Worth," *RISD Views* (Fall 2002), 4-5.

Austin, Nancy. "Defining the *Design* in RISD," RISD *Views* (Spring 2003), 22-23.

Austin, Nancy. *Towards a Genealogy of Visual Culture at the Rhode Island School of Design, 1875-1900.* (Brown University: ProQuest, UMI Dissertation Publishing, 2009). 3370099.

Austin Nancy. "'What a *beginning* is worth': The Women's Centennial Committee of Rhode Island and the Founding of RISD, 1875-1877," (©2002); "'No Honors to Divide': Mrs. Metcalf and the Trustees of the Women's Centennial Commission Fund," (©2004); "The Jones Bequest Lawsuit and the Meaning of a Museum." (©2000). In *Infinite Radius*: a history of the Rhode Island School of Design. ed. Andrew Martinez and Dawn Barrett. (October 2009).

Austin, Nancy. "The Half-Life and After-Life of New Media," (Nov. 2015) *Journal of Contemporary Archival Studies*, Vol. 2, Article 3. (November 2015), 1-30. [http://elischolar.library.yale.edu/jcas/vol2/iss2/3]

Bell, Quentin. *The Schools of Design* (1963).

Biographical History of the Manufacturers and Business Men of Rhode Island (1901).

Blair, Karen. *The Clubwoman as Feminist* (1980).

Bolger, Doreen. *In Pursuit of Beauty* (1986).

Born, Pamela. "The Canon is Cast: Plaster Casts in American Museum and University Collections," *Art Documentation* 21.2 (2002), 8-13.

Brown, Dee. *The Year of the Century: 1876* (1966).

Bryant College: The First 125 Years (1988).

Burns, Sarah. *Inventing the Modern Artist* (1996).

Calvert, Monte. *The Mechanical Engineer in America, 1830-1910: Professional Cultures in Conflict* (1967).

Cheit, Earl. *The Useful Arts and the Liberal Tradition* (1975).

Conn, Steven. *Museums and American Intellectual Life, 1876-1926* (1998).

Curran, Ruth E. "'The City of Sisterly Love'" Women and the 1876 Centennial Exhibition. Department of History, Bryn Mawr. (Unpublished Honors Thesis, 1989).

[Doyle, Sarah E.] *History: RI Woman's Club 1876-1893. Program of Work for Members. Seventeenth Annual Report March 1, 1893* (1893).

Edwards, Steven ed. *Art and Its Histories: A Reader* (1999).

Efland, Arthur. *A History of Art Education* (1990).

Forty, Adrian. *Objects of Desire* (1986).
Foucault, Michel. "Nietzsche, Genealogy, History". In *the Foucault Reader* (1984), 76-77.

Foucault, Michel. "The Subject and Power". Reprinted in H. Dreyfus and P. Rabinow, *Beyond Structuralism and Hermeneutics* (1983), 208-226.

Giedion, Siegfried. *Mechanization Takes Command* (1948).

Gillespie, Mrs. E.D. *A Book of Remembrance* (1901).

Goldstein, Carl. *Teaching Art: Academies and Schools from Vasari to Albers* (1996).

Greene, Welcome Arnold. *Providence Plantations for 250Years* (1886).

Harvey, C. and J. Press. *Art, Enterprise and Ethics: The Life and Work of William Morris* (1996).

Heskett, John. *Industrial Design* (1980).

Ivins, William. *Prints and Visual Communication* (1952).

Korzenik, Diana. *Drawn to Art* (1985).

Kristeller, Paul. "The Modern System of the Arts," *Journal of the History of Ideas*, 203, 205. Reprinted in *Ideas in Cultural Perspective*, ed. P. Wiener and A. Noland (1962), 145-206.

Long, Pamela. "Invention, Authorship, "Intellectual Property," and the Origin of the Patents: Notes Toward a Conceptual History," *Technology and Culture* 32.4 (October 1991).

Lucie-Smith, Edward. *A History of Industrial Design* (1983).

Maass, John. *Glorious Enterprise* (1973).

MacDonald, Anne. *Feminine Ingenuity: Women and Invention in America (*1992).

Mandel, Patricia. "History of the Collection*," Selection VII: American Paintings from the Museum's Collection, c. 1800-1930* (1977).

Manson, Grant Manson, "Wright in the Nursery; The Influence of Froebel Education on the Work of Frank Lloyd Wright," *The Architectural Review* 113 (June 1953).

Manson, Grant Carpenter. *Frank Lloyd Wright to 1910 (*1958).

McCabe's Illustrated Centennial (1876).

McCracken, Grant. *Culture and Consumption* (1988).

McGee, David. "From Craftsmanship to Draftsmanship," *Technology and Culture* 40 (April 1999), 209-236.

McKendrick, Neil et. al. *The Birth of Consumer Society* (1983).

McNeill, Ian ed. *An Encyclopedia of the History of Technology* (1990).

Miller, Daniel. *Material Culture and Mass Consumption* (1987).

Miner, George Leland. *Angell Lane* (1948).

Minor, Vernon. *Art History's History* (2001).

Moxey, Keith. *The Practice of Theory* (1994).

Nichols, George Ward. *Art Education Applied to Industry* (1877).

Pevsner, Nikolaus. *Pioneers of the Modern Movement* (1936).

Piore, Michael and Charles Sabel, *The Second Industrial Divide: Possibilities for Prosperity* (1984).

Podro, Michael. *Critical Historians of Art* (1982).

The Practical Draughtsman's Book of Industrial Design (1853).

Prager, Frank and Gustina Scaglia, *Brunelleschi: Studies of his Technology and Inventions* (1970).

Preziosi, Donald. *Rethinking Art History: Meditations on a Coy Science* (1989).

Preziosi, Donald. "Introduction to Part III," *The Early Years of Art History in the United States* (1993).

Preziosi, Donald. *The Art of Art History: A Critical Anthology* (1998).

Preziosi, Donald. *Brain of the Earth's Body: Art, Museums, and the Phantasms of Modernity* (2003).

Prieto, Laura. *At Home in the Studio: The Professionalization of Women Artists in America* (2001).

Schwartz, Frederic. "Magical Signs: Copyright, Trademarks and 'Individuality," *The Werkbund: Design Theory and Mass Culture before the First World War* (1996), 147-212.

Scranton, Philip. *Endless Novelty: Specialty Production and American Industrialization, 1865-1925* (1997).

Shapiro, Michael. *Child's Garden: The Kindergarten Movement from Froebel to Dewey* (1983).

Singerman, Howard. *Art Subjects: Making Artists in the American University* (1999).

Smyth, Craig and Peter Lukehart. *The Early Years of Art History in the United States* (1993).

Snow, Marilyn. "'Visual Copy Collections in American Institutions," *Art Documentation* (21.2) 2002.

Soussloff, Catherine. *The Absolute Artist: The Historiography of a Concept* (1997).

Stone, Edwin Martin. *A Brief Memoir of Thomas Alexander Tefft* (1869).

Swinth, Kirsten. *Painting Professionals* (2001).

Tolliday, Steven, ed. *The Rise and Fall of Mass Production*, 2 vols. in *The International Library of Critical Writings in Business History* (1998).

Vasari, Georgia. *Lives of the Artists* (first published, 1550).

Whitehill, Walter Muir. *Museum of Fine Arts Boston: A Centennial History* (1970).

Wiseman, Cardinal. *The Identification of the Artisan and Artist and the Proper Object of American Education….The Relation of the Arts of Design with the Arts of Production* (1869).